DOUBLE NO-HIT

Double

No-Hit

JOHNNY VANDER MEER'S
HISTORIC NIGHT
UNDER THE LIGHTS

JAMES W. JOHNSON

University of Nebraska Press | Lincoln and London

© 2012 by James W. Johnson. The statistics
in the appendix are courtesy of Retrosheet.
© Retrosheet. Interested parties may contact
Retrosheet at 20 Sunset Rd., Newark DE 19711.

Library of Congress Cataloging-in-Publication Data

Johnson, James W., 1938–
Double no-hit: Johnny Vander Meer's historic
night under the lights / James W. Johnson.
      p. cm.
Includes bibliographical references.
      ISBN 978-0-8032-7139-5 (pbk.: alk. paper)
1. Vander Meer, Johnny, 1914– 2. Pitchers
(Baseball)—United States—Biography.
3. Baseball players—United States—Biography.
4. No-hitters (Baseball)—History—20th
century. I. Title.
GV865.V36J64 2012   796.357092–dc23   [B]
2011036530

Set in ITC New Baskerville by Kim Essman.
Designed by A. Shahan.

FOR KILEY,
may she always keep
her happy disposition

Kids are always chasing rainbows,
but baseball is a world
where you can catch them.

JOHNNY VANDER MEER

Contents

Introduction

In 1938 a rookie left-hander, Johnny Vander Meer, pitched two no-hitters four days apart. How hard is it to throw back-to-back no-hitters?

The fact that it has been done only once in Major League history ought to convince anyone of its difficulty.

Was it a freak occurrence, a fluke even? Perhaps, but it was a stunning accomplishment nonetheless.

Ask Nolan Ryan how tough it is. He had seven chances and failed. "I don't think it will happen again," Ryan said in 1993. But he admitted that in 1975 after he no-hit the Baltimore Orioles he was trying to match Vander Meer in his next start. "I was definitely trying to throw one," he said. The Milwaukee Brewers' Hank Aaron broke up Ryan's bid for a second consecutive no-hitter with a sixth-inning single. Ryan finished with a two-hitter.

Ironically, Ryan pitched his sixth no-hitter on June 11, 1990, fifty-two years to the day after Vander Meer pitched his first one. In his second outing to try to match Vander Meer, Ryan gave up a leadoff single in the third inning as his first hit. Ryan lost—on June 16, not June 15 like Vander Meer—to the Mariners, 5–0, in Seattle. The Mariners had called the game "Guaranteed No-Hitter Night."

Ask Sandy Koufax. Four chances went for naught. "I never even came close to that [record] . . . unless you call the second inning close," he said. Bob Feller? Three chances that failed. Roger Clemens? He never pitched a no-hitter. Neither did Steve Carlton. Four of the five are Hall of Famers. And the fifth, Clemens? Maybe he'll get elected. Someday.

Great things were expected of Vander Meer after the glory of that double no-hitter. Yet Vander Meer never lived up to expectations. Had it not been for the consecutive no-hitters, he probably would have ended his career as a footnote in baseball history.

Vander Meer, a fireballing left-hander, could have been, and indeed should have been, right up there with Koufax, Feller, and Ryan—among the best the country has ever seen. He had a strong left arm, the body frame and temperament typical of great pitchers, and a pitcher's manager. Yet his career was mediocre at best.

He was twenty-two years old when he went up to the Cincinnati Reds, blessed with a blazing fastball but cursed with lousy control. When his career ended at age thirty-six he was still a hard thrower who had trouble finding the plate.

Vander Meer's career was plagued by injuries, self-doubt, and "the old bugaboo, wildness" as he called it. Taking two years from baseball to serve in the navy during World War II didn't help.

There was nothing in-between about Vander Meer's pitching: he was either very good or very bad. At the top of his game, he was virtually unhittable because he tended to pitch well in important games. But when he was down, teams that didn't matter hit him unmercifully.

Vander Meer pitched most of his career for the Reds and their manager Bill McKechnie. "[Vander Meer] was subject to periods of dazzling brilliance," McKechnie said, "and then he would hit the other extreme and be absolutely ineffective. He beat the tough clubs easily, and he let the easy teams pound him from the box."

Hall of Fame pitcher Chief Bender said Vander Meer "would walk three and strike out three. I can recall him just overpowering hitters. They didn't have [radar] guns in those days, but he had to be in the upper 90s. I guess his delivery was pretty deceptive . . . like a shot coming out of a cannon."

McKechnie never lost faith, even though Vander Meer failed to justify such undying loyalty. How long is too long? Vander Meer ended his career with a 119-121 record, falling far short of Hall of Fame recognition no matter how sterling he'd been for those two amazing games.

Vander Meer, a typical Dutchman, was quiet, unassuming, hardworking, and mild-mannered. He had no close friends on the team, but that doesn't mean his teammates disliked him. He was simply a private person who kept himself distant from others.

Roy Smalley, a teammate on the Chicago Cubs at the end of Vander Meer's career, recalled that once, after a game, he had a flat tire some blocks away from Wrigley Field, and Vander Meer stopped to help him change it. Other than that, Smalley said, Vander Meer stuck to himself and was quiet—so quiet that Smalley couldn't recall much else about him.

Vander Meer lacked a sense of humor. Sportswriters didn't find him a particularly good quote. He didn't seem to have exceptional insights into the game, although he became a relatively successful Minor League manager. He drank little and smoked frequently, as was the custom in those days. He continued to smoke until his dying days. He led a simple life off the field, devoting time to his family and to his passions of hunting and fishing. He didn't seek attention, nor did he avoid it. Most notably, Vander Meer never let those two no-hitters go to his head.

Vander Meer's legacy is that one shining five-day period in his life when he used his overpowering fastball to notch a place in baseball history along with Joe DiMaggio, Lou Gehrig, Bob Feller, Hank Greenberg, Al Simmons, Mel Ott, Carl Hubbell, Lefty Grove, Jimmy Foxx, brothers Dizzy and Paul Dean, and Ted Williams.

Remarkably, Vander Meer achieved this stature while only a rookie pitcher for the Cincinnati Reds.

Standing alone, each of Vander Meer's no-hitters was no

more, and no less, significant than any other that had been pitched until that time. But taken together, back to back, no one has ever duplicated them. Probably no one ever will.

If it hasn't been done in seventy years, it is unlikely to happen again in the next seventy. And even if it does, surely it will never be surpassed.

With more than 170,000 Major League games played from 1900 to 2008, there have been 212 official no-hitters. That's about 1 out of every 800 games—and 1,600 starts by pitchers. This means the average pitcher has about a .000625 chance of throwing a no-hitter in a given start.

In 1985 Michael O'Donnell of the *Chicago Tribune* wrote that the higher the opposing team's batting average, the lower the chance of a pitcher throwing a no-hitter. He noted that only two no-hitters in Major League history were pitched against teams hitting more than .300, one in 1922 and the other in 1929. But then, how many teams have had a combined .300 batting average in a season? What is the chance a pitcher will face two poorly hitting teams back to back, as Vander Meer did? O'Donnell concluded that the probability of Vander Meer pitching consecutive no-hitters was about one in ten million.

The no-hitters gave Vander Meer an immortality few in baseball have achieved. For instance, to this day virtually every time a pitcher throws a no-hitter sportswriters question whether that pitcher will match Vander Meer's record in his next start. Somewhere in a newspaper story or radio or TV broadcast you will read or hear, "He will try to match the record of Johnny Vander Meer, the only pitcher to pitch back-to-back no-hitters."

Sandy Koufax said after the Dodgers' Jerry Ruess threw a no-hitter in 1980, "The next start will be the next start. . . . You always hear, 'Can you pitch two in a row like Johnny Vander Meer.'"

After Cleveland's Dennis Eckersley pitched a no-hitter on May 30, 1977, his manager, Frank Robinson, knew that Vander Meer's name would pop up. Asked about Eckersley's next start,

Robinson replied, "I hope it won't affect him too much. But you know what's going to come up. The old thing. Vander Meer." He added, "Dennis will be reading about it in the papers. I hope he just goes out and pitches." Asked if he would be thinking of challenging Vander Meer's record, Eckersley replied, "No, no, I'm just gonna win. I've had my day. Now I'm just gonna win." Eckersley threw 5⅔ innings in his next outing before giving up a hit.

Except on rare occasions, pitchers who throw no-hitters often have rough outings in their next start. For example, the Red Sox's Jon Lester, who threw one in 2008, gave up a hit to the first batter he faced in his next start. In 2009 Mark Buehrle of the Chicago White Sox pitched a perfect game and then, in his next start, retired seventeen batters in a row before losing the game 5–3. Buehrle did set a Major League record, retiring forty-five batters in a row—the last one in a game that preceded his no-hitter.

Baseball experts agree that pitching a no-hitter takes a psychological and emotional toll, often leading pitchers to need three or four starts before getting back to peak performance.

"What's so hard about it," Feller said, "is the psychological pressure after pitching the first no-hitter. From the first pitch in the second game, you're thinking ho-hitter. I never went past the third or fourth inning of any of mine before I gave up the hit, and it was a relief."

Pitchers swear publicly that they don't think about no-hitters, especially if they've pitched one the game before. Al Leiter, for example, took the mound for the Florida Marlins on May 11, 1996, against the Chicago Cubs after no-hitting the Colorado Rockies. He didn't last long before giving up his first hit against the Cubs. After the game he said, "I made an internal joke when [Leo] Gomez got the single. I said, 'Well, there goes my no-hitter.' I never think no-hitter, even that day. But it was just joking with myself. . . . I really didn't think about Johnny Vander Meer and back to back. That would have been ridiculous."

Asked if he could pitch consecutive no-hitters, Derek Lowe replied after he tossed his first one on April 27, 2002, with the Red Sox, "Oh, hell no. That's like asking Tiger Woods after he shoots a 59 if he thinks he can do it again. . . . How is it going to affect my next outing? I don't want to give up any hits. I think it's that way any time—you don't want to give up any hits or any runs. . . . The chance of this happening again is probably zero."

It might take a fireballer like Sidd Finch, who could throw 168 mph, to match Vander Meer's record. But Finch was a fictional character created by George Plimpton in a legendary April Fool's Day hoax story in 1985.

Pitching a double no-hitter takes more than skill; it takes a strong measure of luck. "I cannot imagine anybody doing that again," said Lonny Frey, who played second base during both of Vander Meer's no-hitters. Former Reds pitcher Joe Nuxhall may have said it best. "It's almost unbelievable, to pitch eighteen innings without allowing a base hit. There are guys, I'm sure, who had better stuff than [Vander Meer]. But I doubt that will be ever duplicated. Certainly, the feat he performed is one of the all-timers, probably the all-timer."

Some have come close. One lost a second consecutive no-hitter on a hit that could well have been an error, in the first inning of the second game. Another fell short in the ninth inning of the second game when, with one out, a ground ball skipped through his legs into center field. That, too, could have been an error.

Dominant pitchers like Koufax, Ryan, and Feller had much better chances, which is why they accounted for fourteen no-hitters among them in just 1,571 starts.

One thing is certain: no-hitters aren't likely to occur with a poor fielding team. They can happen if a pitcher is on a hot streak and runs into a second-division club or one that's slumping at bat—but only if the pitcher has good control and command of all his pitches.

Luck also plays a huge role. Bob Feller may have had some

luck when he pitched three no-hitters, but luck escaped him in twelve other games when he pitched one-hitters.

For a variety of reasons, it may be more difficult today to pitch a no-hitter than in the 1930s. Today's hitters are bigger, stronger, and faster than their 1930s counterparts. Use of steroids has given some players greater strength to knock balls out of the park. Faster runners now beat out more base hits.

Even the higher number of stolen bases today leads to more runs. In 1938, for example, National League teams averaged forty-four stolen bases, while in 2007 they averaged ninety-seven. The American League's use of the designated hitter adds to the difficulty of throwing a no-hitter, with a better hitter replacing the pitcher in the batter's box.

Today's mound is ten inches high, while Vander Meer pitched on a sixteen-inch mound. A higher mound gives pitchers greater leverage when throwing. A lower mound gives the hitter an advantage. In 1938, for example, National League teams averaged 76 home runs; in 2007 they averaged 169.

Artificial turf also leads to more base hits, as batters beat out high-bouncing balls or line drives that infielders might be more likely to grab on grass. Ten fields from the 1970s to the 1990s had artificial turf. Today two do.

Luck can't be overlooked, either. A windy day can keep balls in the park. A bad hop can ruin a no-hitter. Or a bobbled ball can be ruled an error or a hit, depending on the scorekeeper. Umpires may call pitches that work to a pitcher's or a hitter's advantage. The Dodgers' Dale Mitchell struck out looking at a ball that he said was high and outside for the last out of Yankee pitcher Don Larsen's perfect game in the 1956 World Series. Even the Yankees agreed the pitch was a ball. Controversy arose over claims that umpire Babe Pinelli gave Larsen a favorable call knowing that history was at stake.

But luck is not a measure of greatness. Several lucky pitchers have pitched no-hitters but have not gone on to stellar careers. Some top pitchers have never pitched a no-hitter.

As Nolan Ryan noted, "Too many things have to go right to pitch one in the first place, much less two. You need some runs, balls have to be hit right at someone. It takes a lot of luck."

The pressure put on today's pitchers during their next start after a no-hitter shouldn't be discounted. Danny Sheridan, a sports analyst for USA Today and CNN, said that in calculating the chance of a pitcher throwing two no-hitters in a row, "I factor in emotion as well as statistics because of all the media attention a pitcher would get going for a second time." Vander Meer held a strategic advantage over today's pitchers—lack of media attention. He didn't know that no one had ever done it before. He had other distractions to keep him from thinking about it, including pitching baseball's first night game and knowing that his parents, along with five hundred residents from his hometown, were in attendance at the second game.

Hall of Famer Jim Bunning, who threw two no-hitters, put it well. "A no-hitter is a freaky thing. You can't plan it. It's not something you try to do. It just happens. Everything has to come together all on the same day: good control, outstanding plays from your teammates, a whole lot of good fortune on your side, and a lot of bad things for the other guys."

Leiter said it is "nearly impossible" to duplicate Vander Meer's feat because

> there's no rhyme nor reason to the game of baseball. You can have an impeccable game plan and fantastic routine and it doesn't matter: You can be perfect in your execution and still give up a hit. . . . They say Joe DiMaggio's hitting streak is the hardest streak in any sport, but I would argue that throwing back-to-back no-hitters is harder. As a pitcher you are so left out there for uncertainty. As a hitter, you are in control with your execution. How many years have we played baseball? Multiply that by how many games we've played and once upon a time a guy threw back to back no-hitters.

Thousands of baseball players have toiled in the Major Leagues—ranging from those who had "a cup of coffee" to the stars who are selected to the Hall of Fame. And only a handful of the average players, run-of-the-mill if you will, have achieved one shining moment that goes down in baseball lore. Larsen's perfect game was one. Fernando Tatis's two grand slams in one inning in 1999 is yet another. Oh, yes, the two slams were against the same pitcher, Chan Ho Park.

ESPN found Vander Meer's achievement so remarkable that in 2002 it picked the double no-hitters as one of the thirty most memorable moments in baseball after conducting a poll of the media, baseball executives, and baseball historians. Others included Lou Gehrig's farewell speech, Babe Ruth's sale to the Yankees, Jackie Robinson's integrating of baseball, Larsen's World Series perfect game, and Barry Bonds breaking the season home run record. Heady company.

So how does Vander Meer's performance stack up against other immortal records? Records that some said would never be broken include Babe Ruth's sixty home runs. Others are too far out of reach, particularly those in the early 1900s—Cy Young's 749 complete games, for example.

What did Vander Meer think about the longevity of his record? In October 1971 he said that was the question he was asked more than any other. In 1951 Vandy said, "I'd bet that Babe Ruth's home-run record will be broken before mine." He was right on that count. "Well, I think mine and Joe DiMaggio's fifty-six game hitting streak are just about the two roughest records to break," he added. So far he's right on that one, too.

The consensus seems to be that DiMaggio's record is less likely to be broken than Vander Meer's. The Yankee Clipper disagreed. "You can say that a record like [Vander Meer's] will not be broken because someone would have to pitch three no-hitters to break it," he said. "But my record, sure, it'll be broken one day."

In 1969 *Sport* magazine polled three hundred baseball owners, ex-managers, coaches, umpires, scouts, and Hall of Famers asking what were baseball's three greatest achievements. DiMaggio's hitting streak was chosen first and Babe Ruth's sixty home runs second. Vander Meer's no-hitters finished third. Ted Williams's .406 batting average came in fourth, and Larsen's perfect game in the 1956 World Series was fifth.

An undated ESPN poll answered by 5,989 readers on all sports ranked the feats of DiMaggio's hitting streak (30 percent), Cal Ripken's consecutive game record of 2,632 (18.8 percent), and Vander Meer's no-hitters (18.8 percent) as the top three.

In 2006 *Sports Illustrated*'s web page said the ten records least likely to be broken, in no particular order, were:

Cal Ripken's record
Johnny Vander Meer's consecutive no-hitters
Cy Young's 749 career complete games
Owen Wilson's 36 triples in one season
Jack Chesbro's 41 wins in one season
Walter Johnson's 110 career shutouts
Joe DiMaggio's 56-game hitting streak
Nolan Ryan's 5,714 career strikeouts
Rogers Hornsby's .424 average in one season
Rickey Henderson's 1,406 career stolen bases

What sets Vander Meer's effort apart from Ruth's or DiMaggio's is that his teammates were under considerable defensive pressure to help him achieve his no-hitters.

There's no mystery about why Vander Meer doesn't rank among the game's greatest pitchers. He just wasn't sufficiently consistent. But he left his place in history—and it's a story that needs to be told.

Prologue

On June 8, 1938, three days before Johnny Vander Meer was to take the mound against the National League's fifth-place team, the Boston Bees, the Cincinnati Reds' general manager, Warren Giles, had a prophetic dream. "I slept restlessly last night," he told his assistant, Frank Lane. "I was dreaming of Vander Meer pitching a no-hitter."

He may have had good reason to feel that the dream was prophetic because during Vandy's last outing against the New York Giants, on June 5, he was virtually unhittable, throwing a three-hitter against the first-place club. He gave up two hits in the first inning and no more until the ninth, with two outs. Then center fielder Hank Leiber hit a ball off his fists and punched it into right field.

But a no-hitter by a wild-throwing rookie pitcher? Surely it was no more than a dream.

When Vander Meer walked to the mound that June 11, only about ten thousand fans, half of them Knothole Day youngsters, were in attendance at venerable Crosley Field in Cincinnati. Three of them were cousins who had hopped a streetcar and were admitted to the ballpark for a cylindrical cardboard cap from a milk bottle instead of the usual fifty cents. Frank Mathias and his two cousins, Dave and Jim Mathias, "didn't have enough sense to stay once we got there."

What they missed was Giles's dream come true.

Vandy was off to a good start in 1938, racking up a 5-2 won-loss record and leading the league with fifty-two strikeouts when he matched up against the Bees' Danny MacFayden, a curve-ball specialist known as "Deacon Danny." MacFayden, who one sportswriter said looked like "a Harvard botany professor," managed a seventeen-year career in the Major Leagues.

Vander Meer felt sharp that day. Although he had his wildness under control, his fastball lacked its usual zip. But he managed to keep the ball low and away from hitters, forcing them to hit ground balls.

Vandy stuck with his signature windup, rearing back and throwing as hard as he could, his right leg lifted high above his head like it was dangling on a puppet's string as he turned away from home plate. Then the leg would lash forward, his hip would twist, and the ball would explode toward the plate, landing with a loud pop when it hit the catcher's mitt. Batters rarely got a look at the ball until it left his hand, as he hid it in his glove behind his right leg.

Batters were careful not to dig in against Vander Meer for fear of getting hit by one of his high, hard pitches. Vandy once compared himself to Van Lingle Mungo, who he described as a mean pitcher that batters didn't dig in on. "They didn't toe in on me, either, heh heh," Vander Meer said. Boston Red Sox legend Johnny Pesky once described Vandy as "mean."

Vandy retired the Bees in order in each of the first three innings. In the second inning, center fielder Harry "Wildfire" Craft got a good jump on a liner to make a nice running catch on the center-field terrace to rob third baseman Gil English, the sixth batter he faced, of a base hit. A *Cincinnati Enquirer* sportswriter with a sense of drama called it a "spine-tingling, one-handed catch."

In the fourth inning Vandy issued a walk to Gene Moore. On a hit-and-run play Moore took off for second base. Vander Meer got Johnny Cooney to pop up to catcher Ernie Lombardi. Moore, who was almost at second base, tried to stop but slipped. With a quick throw, Lombardi doubled Moore off first. Moore was forced to leave the game when he twisted his ankle on the play.

That same inning Vince DiMaggio smacked one of only four hard-hit balls off the left-hander. DiMaggio lined a ball off Vander Meer's glove, but third baseman Lew Riggs was able to throw DiMaggio out at first on a call that was so close it brought a prolonged argument from Bees manager Casey Stengel.

In the fifth inning Vandy walked Tony Cuccinello, but Lombardi picked him off at first with a snap, sidearm throw that caught him leaning toward second base. "Lom would pick about five to seven guys a year off of first base," Vandy said, "throwing sidearm behind left-handed hitters."

Picking Cuccinello off base evokes memories of a time when Cuccinello pulled the hidden-ball trick on Lombardi. Cuccinello showed Lombardi the ball after he had caught him off second base. Lombardi told Cuccinello, "You tag me and I'll punch you right in the nose." Not surprising, Cuccinello, five foot seven and 160 pounds, didn't test the 230-pound Lombardi. The lumbering catcher walked off the field. No one was going to show him up.

Just about the time Cuccinello was doubled up, the three Mathias cousins decided they had about had enough. They became bored. "Dumb old Boston isn't getting any hits," they grumbled. After a few innings Dave said, "Let's walk down to the [Union Railroad] station and have some fun." So they left the game, not knowing what they left behind.

Later in the fifth inning Vandy walked Gil English, but the Bees stranded him at first, the last runner to reach base against Vander Meer.

The Reds scored the winning run in the fourth when Wally Berger, who had been picked up from the Giants less than a week before, hit a triple and came home on a sacrifice fly by Ival "Goodie" Goodman, who also was known as "Mate" because he had a tendency to call everyone he met "Mate." In the sixth

Lombardi hit a two-run home run that gave the Reds their final margin of 3–0.

As the game moved along, Vander Meer seemed to get stronger. He had strong command of his curve ball, which made his fastball that much more effective. "They were hitting the ball into the ground a lot," Vander Meer said.

In the seventh inning Vandy realized that he had a no-hitter going, in part thanks to Stengel. He and Coach George "High Pockets" Kelly kept shouting from the dugout that Vander Meer had not given up a hit.

Vander Meer had picked up a habit from future Hall of Famer Waite Hoyt, in that when he got to the ninth inning he would tell himself he had twenty good pitches left. "I'd start counting with twenty, then nineteen, and so on. . . . So that gave me a bit of incentive in the last inning that I pushed myself with."

Stengel sent up three right-handed pinch hitters in the ninth, hoping to jinx Vander Meer. Stengel was relying on the strategy that right-handed hitters had a better chance of getting a hit against a left-handed pitcher. One player Stengel left on the bench was left-hander Deb Garms, a .350 hitter who was in the middle of an eighteen-game hitting streak.

The first pinch hitter, Bob Kahle, batting for Rabbit Warstler, grounded to first baseman Frank McCormick, who threw to Vandy, who was covering first, for the out. Then Harl Maggert batted for MacFayden. Vander Meer stared down Maggert, wiped his fingers across his red lettering, and pumped a fastball right by him. Two similar pitches and Maggert was a strikeout victim. A third pinch hitter, right-handed batter Ray Mueller, stepped in for left-hander Elbie Fletcher. Mueller hit the first pitch, topping it down the third base line, where Lew Riggs fielded it and tossed the ball across the diamond to McCormick for the third out.

Vander Meer, a twenty-three-year-old rookie, was in the record book. His teammates carried him off the field on their shoulders, and fans swarmed around the Reds' dugout.

In the 3–0 win Vandy walked three and struck out four while facing only one batter over the minimum. Just five balls were hit out of the infield. It was only the second no-hitter pitched in the National League during the 1930s; the first was by Paul Dean for the Cardinals over Brooklyn on September 21, 1934. At the time a no-hitter wasn't particularly unusual, although Cincinnati newspapers gave it front-page banner headlines. After all, Cincinnati was a relatively small city in those days, and the other most important news, a fire that destroyed 212 buildings, took place halfway round the world in Ludes, Latvia. Not exactly of local interest.

Eighty-three pitchers had pitched a no-hitter before Vander Meer. In addition, the Bees were the worst-hitting team in the Major Leagues with a .245 average. They also scored rock bottom in runs, with 161. "He's a real pitcher," Stengel said about Vander Meer. "You watch him from now on. They'll have trouble beating him."

"I was lucky," Vander Meer said after the game. "I didn't realize that I had a no-hitter in the making until the seventh inning when [Kelly and Stengel] started kidding me about it. I didn't think anything about it then. All I was interested in was a winner, and I was quite certain of that, especially after Lombardi hit that two-run homer in the sixth."

But the best was yet to come for young Mr. Vander Meer.

Nighttime Pageantry 1

Four days after his no-hitter Johnny Vander Meer was expecting to pitch against the seventh-place Brooklyn Dodgers in the first Major League night game in New York. When he walked out of the dugout onto the soft Ebbets Field turf he looked around at the spectacle before him.

Thousands of "haughty gothamites," as one sportswriter called them, were filing into the cramped, thirty-two-thousand-seat stadium. He looked into the twilight to see hundreds more looking down on the field from atop neighboring apartment buildings.

Even though he had pitched a no-hitter in his last start he was only a curiosity that night. The festivities that preceded the game set the stage for what would be a record-setting night.

The Ebbets Field box office had opened at 5:00 p.m. with plenty of seats available. They didn't last long. Forty-five minutes before the scheduled start of the game, 38,748 fans had crammed into the park—on a Wednesday night no less. And 20,000 more were turned away when all the lightbulb-shaped tickets—priced from $1.10 for box seats to $0.55 for the bleachers—were sold.

The unruly fans pushed and shoved their way into the park and into their seats, some of which had already been taken. Scuffles broke out over the seats. Vandy watched in amazement.

"Whether night ball is circus stuff or not," said Jim Mulvey, the Dodgers' executive secretary, "tonight's crowd proves that it's what the public wants."

Teenager Edie McCaslin attended the game with her fiancé.

"We went out to the ballpark, but I was afraid we weren't going to be able to get in," she said. "But we got a place fairly close. The place was jammed. It was a pleasant evening. We sat on the stairs. . . . You couldn't live in Brooklyn without being a Dodger fan. There was electricity to the place that just hit you in the face."

Joining McCaslin was the flamboyant Hilda Chester, armed with her brass cowbells ready to let each and every player know when he did something good or bad. Another was Minnie Ebbets, the former wife of the part-owner and president of the Dodgers. The eighty-year-old woman, severely crippled by arthritis, hadn't been to a game in three years: "When I saw those little towels they put on the backs of the seats I had to laugh when I remembered the bare boards I once had to sit on long ago."

As Vander Meer looked around he spotted a group of about five hundred fans who had traveled thirty miles from his hometown of Midland Park, New Jersey, to honor him for his no-hitter against the Bees. Among them were his parents and his girlfriend, Lois Stewart. "I wish Mom wasn't going to be here tonight," Vander Meer later said he'd mused before the game. "When a fellow pitches a no-hitter, he usually doesn't do very well his next time out. I don't want her to have to sit there and watch me get bombed."

Vandy's hometown newspaper, the *Paterson Morning Call,* prophesied the day before the game. "Watch Johnny Vander Meer repeat his no-hit, no-run game," wrote Bob Whiting. "And don't be too surprised if he does it tomorrow night at Brooklyn to reward his Midland Park and local fans, who will give him a 'day' along with a number of gifts."

In a brief ceremony before the game his family and friends presented Vander Meer with a watch. "According to baseball tradition, anytime you're honored like that by your friends you're supposed to have a bad game," Vandy said. "I was sure I'd be out of there by the third inning."

Even though Reds manager Bill McKechnie didn't tell Vandy he was going to pitch that night until about two hours before the game started, Vander Meer was pretty confident he was going to take the mound. For one, McKechnie religiously stuck to the same rotation of his pitchers, and it was Vander Meer's turn. In addition, Vander Meer's fastball would be harder to hit under the lights. And how could McKechnie not pitch his red-hot rookie when his parents and hometown supporters were on hand?

While playing under the lights was new to New York, it wasn't to the Dodgers' executive vice president, Larry MacPhail. He had picked up the nickname of the Barnum of Baseball because of his entrepreneurial farsightedness and innovative boldness.

MacPhail, a future Hall of Famer, had introduced night baseball to the Major Leagues when he was general manager of the Reds for three years in the mid-1930s, before he moved to the Dodgers in 1937. After a long struggle he convinced club owners to allow him to play seven night games in 1935.

Those games changed the face of the national pastime.

The move to night baseball began with a casual conversation with the Reds' new owner, Powel Crosley Jr., about how to improve attendance at Crosley Field. MacPhail told Crosley that when he was at Columbus in the Minor Leagues, night baseball had attracted more fans.

"Why can't we put in lights at Cincinnati?" Crosley asked.

"Oh, that's out of the question," MacPhail answered.

"Is there any rule against it?" Crosley asked.

"No, but . . ."

"Why don't we try?"

So he did. Once MacPhail was on board with Crosley's idea, he had to sell to other club owners the idea that night baseball would create "another Sunday" during the week—that is, playing games at night would make it possible for working folks to attend games during the week.

But he ran into immediate and adamant opposition from club owners at every turn.

The *New York Times*'s Arthur Daley reported that baseball executives were horrified when MacPhail put forth his proposal. "The man was manifestly mad, a Bolshevik without the slightest regard for the sanctity of their traditions," Daley wrote. "Shades of Abner Doubleday! This wild-eyed radical was asking for permission to introduce night baseball to the big leagues."

Reds historian Lee Allen said MacPhail was looked upon "as something of a charlatan, trying to breathe fresh life into the corpse of the Cincinnati franchise with the methods of a quack."

"That's bush league stuff," said one of the other owners loftily. "It doesn't belong in the big leagues."

"Maybe so," MacPhail responded. "But night baseball has saved the minors from collapse, and the Cincinnati franchise is in such perilous financial condition that it needs extra help. It's almost a case of light up or fold up. Which do you want? I'm only asking for seven night games, one with each club. And I'm only asking it on an experimental basis for one season. If it doesn't hype our gate, as I'm sure it will, I'll abandon it next year."

MacPhail's effort ran into two formidable roadblocks, the New York Giants owner Charles A. Stoneham and Commissioner Kenesaw Mountain Landis. Landis told MacPhail that not in his lifetime would he ever see a baseball game played at night in the Majors.

As he was heading into a meeting with team owners, Stoneham told MacPhail he would never vote for night baseball. MacPhail pleaded, "Do me a favor and listen to my argument before you make up your mind. I make you this promise: If we are permitted to play night games next season, and you are dissatisfied, I'll never use the lights again, no matter how much we invest in them."

It took three hours, but MacPhail and Crosley got them to come around after noting that 70 percent of the Reds' home attendance came on fifteen dates—opening day, Sundays, and holidays. The other National League owners also went along but with several provisions, including a limitation of seven night games, that no lights could be turned on during a game that started in the daytime, and that lights would not be used on Saturdays, Sundays, or holidays.

Stoneham abstained from voting on the Reds' bid for lights but vowed that baseball would never be played at the Polo Grounds at night. The American League refused to go along with what would be the wave of the future. The Washington Senators' Clark Griffith wailed, "MacPhail is making a circus of the game. Night baseball is synthetic; Washington fans will never see it."

"Night baseball is just a fad," said Ed Barrow of the Yankees. "It will never last once the novelty wears off."

Neither were players happy about the lights. Brooklyn pitcher Van Lingle Mungo worried that playing at night would hurt his arm. Said another Dodger pitcher, "The major leagues[, which are] supposed to represent the top of this business, are being turned into a five-and-ten-cent racket by night baseball."

The *New York Post*'s Stanley Frank predicted that night games would be the death of baseball.

Yet many of the players, including Vander Meer, had played night ball in the Minors, where the lighting ranged from bad to awful.

The Reds went ahead with their plans. General Electric installed eight 130-foot towers bearing 614 fifteen-hundred-watt lamps at Crosley Field, at a total cost of $62,000. They were three times more powerful than the lights on any Minor League field.

The first night game was to be played on May 23, 1935, but rain postponed it a day. The next night 20,422 fans saw history in the making. When the lights came on, the crowd let out a collective gasp. Finally, on a cold night, the game began. Radio broadcaster Red Barber remarked from his "catbird seat": "As soon as the lights come on, I knew they were there to stay. The lights were perfect. There were no shadows. Everything was so lovely."

MacPhail never backed away from his support. "Look," he said, "you can read a newspaper out on the field." League president Ford Frick was impressed. "It was swell," he said. "One game, of course, is no criterion, but the players were not handicapped in any way that I could see and I believe we will have more of it in 1936." American League president Will Harridge joined in, commenting that the lighting was "the best I have ever seen in operation. . . . It was the greatest spectacle of modern baseball for several years."

Cincinnati played seven night games that season, drawing 129,991 fans, more than a quarter of the year's total attendance. The 448,000 fans who attended Reds games that year was double the number attending the previous year. The increased attendance, MacPhail said, "meant that we could buy an expensive star every year instead of every three years."

And here was MacPhail introducing night baseball again, this time on June 15, 1938, in Ebbets Field. Again he had to overcome the naysayers, this time his neighbors in New York City. The Giants and the Yankees were incensed because they claimed the Dodgers had agreed that night baseball would be prohibited in the city.

Countered MacPhail in a letter to Giants treasurer Leo Bondy: "The directors of the Brooklyn club advised me there was no contract, 'pact,' or understanding of any kind, nature or description regarding night baseball. If Mr. Bondy can tell us where we can get a couple of pitchers, we would appreciate his assistance. Otherwise, we suggest he confine his efforts to running the Giants. The only 'pact' my directors know anything about is an understanding engineered by Mr. Bondy several years ago that has resulted in depriving New York fans of all broadcasts of baseball games."

The newspapers couldn't pass up the opportunity to have a little fun with the Dodgers and night baseball. Dan Parker of the *New York Daily Mirror* wrote that "the Dodgers should learn to play baseball in the daytime before attempting the more difficult task of playing it in the evening, which is reserved for more pleasant pastimes in Brooklyn."

Chimed in Bob Ray of the *Los Angeles Times*, "Brooklyn will put in arc lights at Ebbets Field and go in for night baseball. There are those who contend Dodger baseballers have always played in the dark."

Giants secretary Aloysius McGonigle Brannick said, "Brooklyn—the City of Dreadful Night! You've seen those Dodgers play in daylight. Imagine what they'll be after dark! The citizens should be warned away. It ain't safe. A man might go there and die laughing."

But Brooklyn officialdom was enthusiastic about playing under the lights. The Dodgers' house organ, "Dodger Doings," said about the new lighting system that a man could sit on second base and read a newspaper under lights that were ten times brighter than an ordinary reading lamp in his home. It said the lighting system would light a highway for a distance of forty-four miles or would supply illumination for nine thousand city blocks. "The cost of operating the plant for one game is approximately the same as the cost of lighting fifteen hundred homes for the same period," it said, noting that more than thirty thousand bolts, two miles of pipes, and fifteen miles of cable were used to complete the job.

MacPhail called the lighting system "the best lighting plant [that] science can produce and the best money can buy."

The *Brooklyn Eagle* took note that Vandy pitched pretty well at Minor League parks with lights. Under the headline "No-Hit Vander Meer Mr. Big under Bulbs," the newspaper noted that Vandy had led all of pro baseball with 295 strikeouts in 214 innings for Durham in 1936, and most of those games had taken place under the lights. The paper also noted that the Reds had won both previous 1938 evening contests, the first of which was won by Vander Meer 2–1 against the Cardinals. In addition, the Dodgers had lost all four of their night games dating back to 1935. Vander Meer threw nine innings against the Dodgers in 1938, beating them 4–1 on June 1.

Vandy was used to pitching under the lights in the Minors, saying he had never played day ball until he got to the Major Leagues. "I supposed you figure that any pitcher with something real fast is practically invincible after dark," Vander Meer said. "Well, it doesn't work that way in the major leagues." Vander Meer pointed out that in the Minors pitchers could throw a fastball by the hitters, especially when the ballpark had an inferior lighting system. But in the Majors, he said, better lighting took away the pitcher's advantage. Vandy professed to prefer pitching in daytime. "I do not like the cold and the damp after dark," he said.

As it turned out, Vander Meer's record under the lights was twelve wins and thirteen losses in the Minors, so any suggestion that the lights helped him on his second no-hitter was unfounded.

On game day—at 3:00 a.m. to be exact—General Electric officials tested all 615 of the lights, which provided light intensity of ninety-two million candlepower. MacPhail's telephone rang off the hook with neighbors complaining they were unable to sleep because of the illumination in their windows. Nonetheless, night games proved a rousing success in Brooklyn. The Dodgers' first five night games drew 153,498 fans, an average of just over thirty thousand per game, compared with four thousand for day games. In the four preceding seasons, the most the Dodgers drew was 489,618 fans during the 1936 season. With the addition of lights, attendance soared to 663,087 in 1938—to watch a seventh-place team.

The *New York Times*'s John Kieran prophesied about that first night game in Brooklyn: "It seems to this observer that Laughing Larry [MacPhail] is taking a wild chance in selecting Cincinnati as the guest club for this first night game in Brooklyn. [Or perhaps he was nostalgic about the first night game in Cincinnati.] Mild Will McKechnie might send Johnny Vander Meer to the mound against them if he was in the mood to put over a mean trick. The last time out this Vander Meer didn't [allow] the Boston Bees a single hit in broad daylight. What chance would Brooklyn have against him after the sun went down?"

The late start of the game forced Vander Meer to warm up, sit down, warm up again, and then sit some more. He estimated he threw more than 225 pitches that night, 50 of them before the game began. (Pitchers weren't on a pitch count in those days.)

The ushers were having trouble controlling the crowd. People were sitting in the aisles, and the public address announcer kept telling everyone the game wouldn't start until the aisles were cleared. "I remember hearing him say that over and over, and getting up and down to warm up," Vander Meer said.

At one point the bleacher bums became restless, clapping their hands in unison until one of the bands marched onto the field. These were the same kind of Brooklyn fans—why would they be any different?—who on opening day rained cushions down on Giants outfielders, prompting the announcer to ask, "Will the bleacher fans please refrain from throwing cushions?" The fans responded by throwing more cushions. Then the announcer caught himself and asked, "Will the fans please not throw any more cushions on the field?" No more cushions flew, for apparently the Brooklyn fans were not privy to the definition of *refrain*.

While the fans settled into their seats—and even the aisles—they were treated to fireworks, two fife-and-drum corps, and a band. MacPhail had paid Jesse Owens, winner of four gold medals in the Berlin Olympics in 1936, the handsome sum of $4,000, an amount equivalent to $50,160 in 2008 dollars, to put on a track exhibition.

Owens raced against the Dodgers' fastest player, Ernie Koy, with Koy getting a ten-yard head start. "I got the jump on the gun," said Koy, a former standout football player at the University of Texas. "That helped me a whole lot. The guy didn't whistle me down, so I just kept going."

The Dodgers gave Koy a fifty-dollar bonus for beating Owens. Years later Koy said baseball promoters wanted him to race Owens again, but he declined. "I told them if you could beat Owens once, you'd better let it ride," he said.

In a broad-jump exhibition Owens leaped twenty-three feet eight inches. Owens also raced the Dodgers' Gibby Brack in the 120-yard low hurdles, which Brack won. The only trouble was that Brack didn't have to clear the ten hurdles that Owens did. One sportswriter said that Brack "should have given Owens a handicap."

During the festivities home run king Babe Ruth, who had been out of baseball for three years, ducked into the Reds' dugout to congratulate Vandy on his no-hitter against Boston. Wearing a Cincinnati cap and dressed nattily in a double-breasted suit, Ruth told the young left-hander, "Nice going, kid."

After Vandy and Ruth chatted briefly Ruth ambled into the box seats, where he was spotted by one of the fans. "It's Babe," he cried out, and Ruth was surrounded by fans. "Hi-ya kid," Ruth said, using the name he gave everyone because he was lousy at remembering names. "Hey, d'you know that in twenty-three years in baseball, this will be the first time I ever watched a game in Ebbets Field?"

MacPhail was looking down from his seat high in Ebbets Field and noticed the crowd around Ruth. Ever the showman, MacPhail announced then and there that Ruth would be the Dodgers' new first base coach for the rest of the season. MacPhail grabbed the public address microphone and yelled, "Babe Ruth belongs in baseball, and so to prove that I mean what I say, Ruth will be in uniform tomorrow here in Ebbets Field." Ruth had been retired from baseball for three years.

It was unlikely Ruth was unaware that he would be the Dodgers' new first base coach. He had always wanted to be a manager, and he hoped to replace Burleigh (Boily, the Dodger fans called him) Grimes. That never happened. Knowing that Ruth could attract fans because he still was the biggest name in baseball, MacPhail talked Ruth into hitting balls out of the park during batting practice. He paid Ruth $15,000 for the rest of the season. In his debut with the Dodgers on June 19, twenty-eight thousand fans showed up, lured by a doubleheader with the Cubs and by the Babe.

The *Sporting News*, which called itself "The Baseball Paper of the World," let it be known in its June 23 edition which event it thought was the most important by running the story of Ruth's return to baseball on its front page while relegating Vander Meer's second no-hitter to the third page.

Finally, at 8:35 p.m., the Ebbets Field lights were turned on. But they took forty-eight minutes to become fully illuminated. At exactly 9:23 p.m., it was time for Vander Meer to make his own history. The temperature was sixty-two degrees with 84 percent humidity when he took the mound. Cool and humid. Vander Meer wasn't wild about pitching in cool weather, but he had other things to worry about.

He was on his way to accomplishing something that had never been done on a baseball field then and that may never happen again. It was a feat so unique that it almost relegated that three-ring circus of a night to a footnote in baseball history.

2 First Inning

During the winter break after the 1937 season, MacPhail eagerly went about acquiring players who could make the Dodgers a ball club that would rise to the top of the National League. He made several moves for players who he felt would knock the cover off the ball.

"Why, we'll have six .300 hitters in our lineup this year," he told sportswriters as spring training opened.

> Sure. Now, look. You can count on [Dolph] Camilli, can't you? He'll hit plenty off that right-field wall—or over it—in Brooklyn. You can count on Babe Phelps. He can powder the ball. Maybe Buddy Hassett won't be the best outfielder in the league this year, but we all know that he'll hit. I think he'll be a good outfielder, given a little time. [Hassett was being shifted from first base to make room for Camilli.] But everyone knows he can hit. Then we have Heinie Manush, a great hitter. He hit .333 last year. Of course we don't figure Heinie is going to play every game. He'll need a rest now and then. But we have [future Hall of Famer] Kiki Cuyler to stick in there, and Cuyler looks well this spring. . . . Well, this [Goodwin "Goody"] Rosen in center field, he's a better hitter than he gets credit for. He'll hit close to .300. And I figure Cookie Lavagetto may get up there, too. He's still a kid, you know. He's improving. Hit .282 last year; oughta do better this year. We'll show 'em some hitting.

It didn't work out that way. Camilli, Cuyler, and Hassett fell far below expectations. Manush would be waived in May. Only Phelps, Lavagetto, and Rosen lived up to their billing. To top it off, none of those players was going to do well that night off Mr. Vander Meer.

When the lights became bright enough start the game, big Max Butcher took the mound for the Dodgers. Butcher stood six feet two inches tall and weighed 220 pounds, an extraordinary size for a man in those days. "Max's eyes were always blinking, and the guys used to say that he pitched between blinks," teammate Buddy Hassett said. It was the first time Vander Meer would take the mound against the hard-throwing right-hander.

Butcher, twenty-seven, had a 4-2 record and was facing the National League's top hitting team with a .283 average. Defensively the Reds and the Dodgers were tied for third with a .973 team fielding percentage.

First up for the Reds was second baseman Lonny Frey, who was batting .267. Frey was hitting left-handed this season after spending the first five years of his career as a switch hitter. The change hadn't helped, as Frey had been averaging about .277 during the previous seasons.

Frey, whose real first name was Linus, after a Roman bishop, played for the Dodgers from 1933 to 1936. Also called Junior because he was five feet ten and 160 pounds, Frey had made fifty-one errors in 1936. Brooklyn fans were unmerciful toward Frey, subjecting him to boos and catcalls on a daily basis. It didn't take "big ears" for him to hear the hecklers. "Hey, genius," someone bellowed at the Dodger shortstop. "What ya got the glove for? A decoration?" From the $1.10 seats in cozy Ebbets Field you could see Frey redden.

Dodger manager Casey Stengel often benched him, and the newspapers were full of talk about trading him. One unidentified Dodger teammate said, "When they roast a ballplayer like that, a fellow might as well root to be traded. No one with any sensibilities at all can listen to that kind of a roar and not get the jitters and become ten times worse."

That winter Frey was traded to the Chicago Cubs, where he was a spot player for the 1937 season, getting into seventy-eight games and batting .278. He played shortstop, second base, third base, and even the outfield. He was shipped off to the Reds in February 1938.

When Bill McKechnie took over as manager of the Reds in 1937 he quickly saw that the team needed a vastly improved defense. McKechnie always had been a defensive-minded manager, and he wasn't about to change. Having observed Frey play shortstop, McKechnie realized his arm was too weak for the long throw to first base. McKechnie felt that Frey's concern with his poor fielding was affecting his overall game, so he put Frey at second base, where his fielding and hitting improved to the point that he may have been the best second baseman in the National League at the time. Frey made the All-Star team in 1939.

Not surprisingly, Frey played particularly hard against the Dodgers, who had touched off his anger by giving up on him. He had been involved in two fights with Dodgers players since leaving the club. Those same Dodger fans that had been hard on him didn't let up when he returned to Ebbets Field on Vandy's big night.

Frey, twenty-seven, had a good sense of the strike zone. In 607 at bats in 1936 he struck out only fifty-seven times. He led off with a single to right field.

Left fielder Wally Berger batted second. The Reds had acquired him nine days earlier from the Giants, where he played in only sixteen games, and he was hitting .462 since joining his new team. In eight years in the big leagues Berger never hit below .285, four times hitting more than .300.

Berger, thirty-two, had played for McKechnie and the Boston Braves from his rookie year in 1930 until 1936. When McKechnie moved to the Reds he wanted Berger back, so he traded weak-hitting infielder Alex Kampouris for him. At six feet two and almost two hundred pounds, Berger possessed a raw power that saw him set Major League standards in home runs and RBIs for rookies when he smacked thirty-eight home runs and drove in 119. In the next seven years he belted 173 home runs. Butcher struck Berger out for the first out of the inning.

Next up was right fielder Ival Goodman, another power hitter despite his relatively small size. Goody, twenty-nine, stood five feet eleven and weighed 170 pounds and averaged almost thirteen home runs per season during his first three seasons in the Majors. Butcher pitched too carefully to Goodman, who was hitting .309, and walked him.

With men on first and second, Butcher faced cleanup hitter Frank McCormick, who was batting .348, third in the league. Buck (after the big-game hunter Frank Buck) was in his first full season in the Major Leagues. He first came up in 1934 at the age of twenty-three but didn't last long, logging five hits in sixteen at bats. He was sent to the Minors before being called up again in 1937, when he played in twenty-four games and hit .325. After that he was there to stay and became a Reds mainstay for the next eight seasons. He finished his career in 1948 with a .299 batting average, eight All-Star Game appearances, and one Most Valuable Player Award.

In his thirteen-year career, encompassing 5,723 at bats and 6,207 plate appearances, the slugging first baseman had just 189 strikeouts—34 fewer whiffs than Diamondbacks slugger Mark Reynolds achieved in only 578 at bats during 2009 alone. While McCormick struck out only seventeen times that year, neither did he walk much—just eighteen times. He liked to swing the bat, often swinging at the first pitch. "I learned early that pitchers tried to sneak a good one by you to get ahead in the count. I didn't let it go by," he said.

His single season total for hits in 1938 and 1939, doubles in 1940, and RBIs in 1939 and 1940 still place him in the top ten in Reds history. He played eight years for Cincinnati, during which he led the team in RBIs seven times, in batting average six times, in slugging average five times, in home runs four times, and in on-base percentage twice.

But McCormick failed this time, hitting a ground ball to Cookie Lavagetto at third, who forced Goodman at second as Frey moved up to third.

That brought up catcher Ernie Lombardi, who was second in the league in batting with a .359 average. He put good wood to the ball, rarely striking out—fourteen times that year, to be exact. He averaged just twenty-three strikeouts a year in his seventeen-year career. Lombardi's lifetime hitting average was .306. The thirty-year-old accumulated 190 home runs, 1,792 base hits, and 990 RBIs. His slugging average was .460. He was voted into the Hall of Fame posthumously in 1986, after Warren Giles did his best to keep him out of the hall while he was alive because of a long-standing spat over his salary.

As well as Lombardi could hit, he was known as one of the slowest men ever to play in the Major Leagues. One observer said he was so slow that he looked like a man carrying a piano "and the fellow tuning it." Another said Lombardi was so slow he was thrown out trying to stretch a double into a single.

Believe it or not, there was a slower player in Major League Baseball. He was James Hogan, who was nicknamed Shanty because he was built like a small hut. He stood six one and weighed 240 pounds. Hogan played thirteen years for three teams and stole six bases. Lombardi stole eight in seventeen seasons. Hogan was washed up by 1937 and released by the Washington Senators, so in 1938 Lombardi was the newly crowned slowest player in the Majors.

Said Vandy, "He was a seven-second man to first base," in a profession where 4.3 seconds from home to first was average for a right-handed batter. "The infielders would play him twenty-five feet back on the outfield grass. Billy Herman always played him thirty feet behind second base." And they still could throw him out at first base.

Lombardi told Pee Wee Reese (a shortstop for the Dodgers and another Hall of Famer), "You had been in the league for five years before I realized you weren't an outfielder."

In a 1935 game against the Phillies, Lombardi had a chance to hit doubles in five consecutive trips to the plate to set a Major League record. On his third at bat Lombardi hit a ball off the outfield wall so hard that he was held to a single. Another time, in the Polo Grounds, he hit a ball under a stairwell 483 feet away and still only managed a triple. He led the National League in hitting into double plays four times.

Lombardi swung the heaviest bat in baseball, using an overlapping golfers' grip on a thirty-six-inch-long bat that weighed forty-two ounces. *New York Times* sportswriter Arthur Daley wrote, "When Lom would grasp a bat with that interlocking grip of his, his bat looked like a matchstick. And the ball would ricochet off it like a shell leaving a howitzer."

He would hit vicious line drives that put fear into every pitcher. He once hit a liner that broke three fingers on the glove hand of Cubs pitcher Larry French. "I thought he might hurt me, even kill me, with one of those liners," Carl Hubbell said.

"If he were playing today, on [an] artificial surface, I don't know where the infielders would play him," Hall of Famer Billy Herman recalled in 1986. "The ball comes off there like a rocket, and the way Lombardi hit it he might kill an infielder today. He could hit a ball as hard as anybody I ever saw, and that includes [Babe] Ruth and [Jimmy] Foxx."

It's probably just an urban legend that Lombardi belted the "longest" homer in Major League history by hitting a ball over the fence at Cincinnati's Crosley Field and into the back of a pickup truck. The truck didn't stop for thirty miles.

When Lombardi came up to the Majors with the Dodgers in 1931, a sportswriter wrote that "Ernest Lombardi travels light. He carries nothing but a blue serge suit, a well-worn cap, a small leather bag, the biggest schnozzola ever seen in baseball circles and a .370 batting average. . . . He weighs 220 pounds right now, but he isn't fat. He stands six-foot-two and his hands are like two enormous hams hanging at the end of his arms." His manager, Wilbert Robinson, called him Lombago because he could never remember Lombardi.

His teammates, who loved him, lent him other nicknames, including "Schnozz," "Bocci," "Dogs" because of his tired feet, "The Cyrano of the Iron Mask," "Big Horn," "Big Slug" because of the way he slugged the ball, and "Lom." He was big-hearted and a soft touch, often handing out five-dollar bills and telling teammates to go out and have a good time.

The Cyrano name came because women adored him, and he had a proboscis that stuck out of his mask. He also had big feet and tree-trunk-like legs. Women would shriek with joy when Lombardi made an appearance. "There was a Sinatra-like adulation of Lom that affected women of all ages, not just bobby-soxers, and after each game they would gather [and wait] to see their hero emerge in street clothes," wrote Lee Allen in his 1948 history of the Cincinnati Reds. The painfully shy Lombardi would stay in the locker room until they left. He remained a bachelor until he was thirty-six.

Sportswriter Roger Kahn, reminiscing about going to games in Ebbets Field as a youth, remembered Lombardi in the compact park where interplay between players and fans was common. When one of the fans shouted, "Hey, Schnozz, pick up your cap so we can see your big nose," Lombardi grinned and raised the bill of the cap. "That nose," Kahn wrote, "could well have startled Cyrano."

Now standing in against Butcher, Lombardi lofted a fly ball to center fielder Ernie Koy, leaving Frey and McCormick stranded.

Bottom of the First 3

It's likely that the no-hitter against the Bees was still on Vander Meer's mind, because it was the last game he'd pitched. But he also had to focus on this game because the Dodgers were a much better hitting club than the Boston Bees, who were last in the Major Leagues with their .245 batting average.

Despite their 21-28 record, which put them in seventh place in the National League, the Dodgers were batting .264. Three starters were hitting over .300, including Lavagetto, whose .360 batting average was leading the league. A fourth player, Goody Rosen, was hitting .299, but he didn't start that night.

Manager Grimes decided to go with the odds by using right-handed hitters against the left-hander Vander Meer. The left-hand-hitting Rosen had broken up two no-hitters earlier in the year. He hit a single off right-hander Hal Schumacher, who didn't allow another hit in a 1–0 victory over the Dodgers on April 24. Rosen singled off the Cardinals' Bill McGee, another right-hander, in the sixth inning for the Dodgers in a 2–1 loss to the Cardinals on May 17.

But how was Grimes to know whether Rosen could have had a third chance? Even when Grimes saw that Vander Meer was no-hitting the Dodgers, he still used Rosen only as a pinch runner.

Twenty-five-year-old Rosen was having a solid year, hitting .301. Perhaps Grimes's pitcher's mentality led him to make the decision to keep Rosen on the bench. Grimes had been a terrific pitcher, the last of the legal spitball throwers. He won 190 games in the 1920s, 270 overall with a 3.53 ERA in a nineteen-year career with seven teams, mostly with the Dodgers. He was inducted into the Hall of Fame in 1964.

Vandy not only had to face a good fielding team, but he was pitching in a terrific hitter's park, the small Ebbets Field. The cramped and colorful park was built for $750,000 on a garbage dump three miles from the Manhattan Bridge in an area known as Pigtown because pigs feasted on the waste each morning. It opened in 1913 with seats for twenty-five thousand fans before a second deck was added to bring seating to thirty-two thousand. Every seat in the house was close to the action, so close that the players could hear the heckling from the stands.

The distance down the left-field line was 365 feet, where the fence stood just shy of 10 feet high. The wall was 20 feet high in center field, which was 402 feet from home plate. The right-field fence was 297 feet down the field line, where the wall stood 38 feet high. Line drives would carom off 289 weird angles on the three walls, which were laden with advertisements. The scoreboard stuck out 5 feet from the center-field wall at a forty-five-degree angle.

In 1931 the owner of a clothing store put an advertisement at the bottom of the right-field scoreboard. Abe Stark's sign said, "Hit Sign, Win Suit," promising a new suit to any batter who hit the sign on the fly. No one did it for six years, until Dodger shortstop Woody English smacked a double off the wall. The way balls came off the wall with its many angles baffled visiting outfielders. But the angles weren't going to bother the Reds on this no-hitter night.

Not only were the Dodgers good hitters, they might have been smarter than most ball clubs. The first three batters that Vander Meer faced that night had attended college. But they weren't going to outsmart Vander Meer, a high school dropout.

Vandy was happy old reliable Ernie Lombardi was behind the plate when he went out to the mound. Any pitcher will tell you that much of his success has to be shared with his catcher, and Lombardi was his battery mate in his no-hitter against the Bees.

It's not necessarily how good a catcher is at fielding but rather the pitches he calls, how well he gains the pitcher's confidence, and how he settles down his pitcher in tight spots. Lombardi often caught both games of a doubleheader.

If Vander Meer was pitching the second game, Lombardi quickly wore down. He would get exhausted chasing Vander Meer's wild pitches. He often would grab errant pitches with his bare hand.

Shortstop Eddie Joost recalled that Lombardi's hands were so big each could hold seven baseballs. "He would stick out that big paw of his and catch bare-handed, spit out a wad of tobacco, and throw the ball back to Vander Meer."

Lombardi led the National League in passed balls nine times. He was too slow to go after low pop-ups, bunts, or balls that got a short distance away. But he blocked the ball well, and he had those good hands. He also could pick off or double up runners on base with snap throws from a crouch or after catching a foul ball. When he threw, the ball had a natural tendency to sink just as it reached the base, making it easier for infielders to tag out runners.

As the game began, Vander Meer must have had trouble putting his previous no-hitter behind him. The Flatbush crowd, always one of the noisiest and rowdiest, wouldn't let him forget it. When he took the field, the partisan crowd was all over him. Camilli recalled of the Brooklyn fans: "All they cared about was their family, their job, and the Dodgers. And I don't know which one was the most important."

As Vandy went into his four-stage windup—one sportswriter called it his "rocking chair"—fans would chant "one" when he leaned forward, "two" as he raised his hands over his head, "three" for the high kick of his right leg, and "four" as he propelled forward and released the ball. It seemed to faze the batters more than Vander Meer. "I paid no attention to the fans when they began to chant. . . . When the fans counted like that they helped me keep the rhythm. Then when they saw their batters were going down, they stopped."

The first batter he faced, Kiki Cuyler, was at the end of an outstanding career. He was one of only four players in the Major Leagues who were at least thirty-eight years old. Jimmy Dykes, at forty, was the oldest player. The Harrisville, Michigan, native was in his seventeenth season. The free-swinging right fielder's real first name was Hazen; his middle name, Shirley. He picked up the nickname Kiki from a shortening of his surname to Cuy, pronounced *Ki*. It is said that he stuttered when he spoke his last name, hence Kiki. Another story had it that when he would dash in for a short fly ball the shortstop would holler "Cuy," which would be echoed by the second baseman. Sportswriters who heard the "Cuy Cuy" turned it into Kiki on the sports pages.

Cuyler had a lifetime .321 batting average—he hit over .300 ten times—but he was hitting just .245 in his first year with the Dodgers and his final year in baseball. The daring, line drive–hitting base runner, one of the fastest in the National League, had also played for the Cubs, the Reds, and the Pirates. Cuyler, who had attended the U.S. Military Academy at West Point, was a playing coach in his final years.

Cuyler was instrumental in the Pittsburgh Pirates' win over the Washington Senators in the 1925 World Series, with a game-winning home run in the second game. In Game Seven he hit a two-run double in the eighth inning off Walter Johnson. He led the National League in stolen bases four times and had 328 in his career. He hit in ten consecutive at bats in 1925, setting a National League record. In 1929 he stole forty-three bases, a mark not surpassed until 1960 by Maury Wills.

In six times at bat against Vander Meer during his career, Cuyler failed to get a hit. On this night Vandy got Cuyler to fly out to Goodman for the first out.

The Dodgers' number two hitter, Pete Coscarart, was a rookie from Escondido, California. During spring training he was one of MacPhail's pet projects. "He's a Basque [he was known as "The Bounding Basque"], a brother of Joe who used to be with the Boston Bees," MacPhail said. "This boy may hit. He's probably pressing a bit now—anxious to stay in the big league—so he isn't hitting with his natural swing."

Apparently Coscarart never did hit well, because he was sent down to the Minors early in the season and had been called up only three weeks earlier. He was getting a rare start ahead of regular Johnny Hudson, a day before his twenty-fifth birthday. Perhaps the Dodgers could have used Hudson's bat in the lineup, since he was hitting .268. Coscarart was better known for his glove than his bat. The next year he was considered the best defensive second baseman in the National League. He was currently hitting .172 with ten hits. He too was a former college student, having been selected from San Diego State Teachers College.

Coscarart may be best remembered for his efforts in 1946 to form a players union that could negotiate pension benefits. He always believed that effort resulted in his being shipped to the Minor Leagues the year before pension benefits were adopted. "There's no way of proving it, but I've always felt I was cheated," he said in 1996. He never received a baseball pension, but neither did he stop fighting for one for himself and others in a similar situation, until his death in 2002.

Coscarart, who would go 5 for 16 against Vandy in his career, struck out for the second out.

Vander Meer almost gave up a hit to the third batter, John Aloysius "Buddy" Hassett, one of three left-handers hitting against the southpaw Vander Meer. Hassett was hitting .256 that season, with no home runs. The twenty-seven-year-old left fielder from New York had moved to the outfield from first base when the Dodgers acquired Dolph Camilli in the spring. One sportswriter noted that Hassett was the cousin of Honey Hassett, a well-known New York model. The writer opined that perhaps Hassett "could use a little of her grace and poise around the bag."

Maybe so, but Hassett could sing; he was an Irish tenor called the Bronx Thrush. Hassett sang in choir at the Paulist church on

Fifty-Ninth Street in New York as a youngster before moving to the Bronx. His father ran the Shamrock Democratic Club and would have parties there, at which Hassett would sing. "I didn't have any formal lessons," he said.

When he played semipro ball he would often sing to entertain fans when it began to rain. The team's manager would hand him a megaphone and ask him to sing to keep people in the stands. "Once in awhile, it worked," he said.

From 1936 to 1938 Hassett sang in stage shows between movies at the downtown Brooklyn Strand, often belting out "When Irish Eyes Are Smiling." But on June 15, 1938, with Vandy on the mound, Hassett would be singing the blues.

Hassett, who also was college educated, having attended Manhattan College, played seven seasons, finishing up with the Boston Bees. He was a .292 career hitter known for getting his bat on the ball. Never in a season did he strike out more than twenty times. Vander Meer didn't get him on strikes, either. In Hassett's career, he was 2 for 11 against Vander Meer.

Hassett hit a pitch back to the box that Vandy jabbed at, deflecting it to second baseman Frey, who threw him out.

A Second Chance 4

Vander Meer almost didn't get his opportunity to achieve baseball immorality when he came down with a near-fatal illness in 1928, not long after he became a teenager.

John Samuel Vander Meer was born November 2, 1914, in Prospect Park, New Jersey, to deeply religious immigrant parents. Jacob and Kathy Vander Meer came to the United States in their early teens from Holland. It was only natural that Vander Meer in his Major League years would earn the nickname "The Dutch Master." He had an older brother, Martin, and a younger sister, Garberdina.

He grew up in Midland Park, New Jersey, population twenty-one hundred—80 percent of whom were of Dutch ancestry. The town was situated along the Passaic River, about thirty miles from New York City. The Vander Meers resided at 43 Rea Avenue in a simple, white, two-story frame house. They were blue-collar folks with strong family values who raised chickens in their back yard.

Johnny received his first baseball after he won a spelling bee in the first grade at the Christian Reform Church School. His father, the son said, "was not interested in sports, and being an immigrant . . . he was only interested in one thing: work." Johnny was almost eight years old when he took an interest in baseball, listening to the 1922 World Series when the New York Giants swept the Yankees and Babe Ruth. At the age of ten he began playing ball as a first baseman for his school team.

The first baseball field Johnny played on was referred to as Stumps Oval. The boys had cleared trees from a field to create a diamond. Most baseball fields were oval-shaped in those days. The youngsters cut down the trees as close to the ground as they could, but low stumps still stuck up. Each morning before a game the boys would prepare the field, raking and hoeing to smooth it as best they could. They even built a rudimentary grandstand.

"Back then there weren't many choices of things to do," Vander Meer reminisced. "Some kids wanted to be firemen, some kids wanted to be policeman, and I just wanted to play ball."

He played baseball every chance he got—in the streets, in the fields, at school. "That's all I did. Ate it, drank it, slept it. Most of the boys at that time wanted to be big leaguers." Johnny's boyhood friend, Dick Jeffer, remembered, "If you owned a glove, you were on the team." Jeffer was Vandy's battery mate but never moved past sandlot ball because he couldn't hit the curve.

Johnny quit high school before he even started when he came down with peritonitis. In the summer of 1928 he felt a deep pain in the right side of his abdomen. His stomach was bloated, and he had chills and a fever along with nausea and vomiting. He felt weak; his skin was pale and cold. The diagnosis was a serious disorder caused by an inflammation of the two-layered membrane lining the abdominal cavity, most likely caused by bacteria. Peritonitis infection can spread to the organs in the stomach area and prove fatal.

In Johnny's day no drugs been developed to combat the infection. Doctors told Johnny's parents that there was a slim chance the youngster would live if they could localize the infection.

The physicians were successful, which allowed them to operate. "I suppose it was the Lord's will that I was to survive," Vander Meer recalled. The ailment continued to bother him off and on during his entire baseball career, forcing him to cut back on the time he spent on the field.

Johnny stayed eight weeks in the hospital and five more at home, long after his first year of high school had started.

"Through those hot August days when I lay almost rigid on a hospital cot," he said, "I didn't know whether I'd ever see another baseball game, much less play in one."

One story has it that instead of returning to school so late in the year he decided to take a job his father got him at the United Piece Dye Works in nearby Hawthorne, New Jersey, where his father was employed for his entire working life in America. Young Johnny served as an apprentice engraver for $18.50 a week and played ball after his shift ended.

In another story, when it came time for Vandy to go to high school, he wanted to attend a nearby school, but his parents wanted him to go to Eastern Christian School or go to work. He chose work. While he was generally respectful of his parents' religious wishes, Vander Meer wasn't much of a churchgoer in his adult life.

Johnny wasn't about to spend his life working in a factory, though. Although he had been advised to take it easy after his hospitalization, "I cheated a little bit, just like any kid would and played [baseball] anyway."

During his teens Johnny developed into a strong young man. He weighed 110 pounds at age fourteen and shot up to 175 by the time he was seventeen. "I had that God-given arm," he said. "Nobody can teach you how to throw the ball hard. Nobody can teach you how to run fast."

Johnny had a hero to emulate. Contrary to several printed statements that his idol was Babe Ruth, Vander Meer most admired future Hall of Fame pitcher Carl Hubbell, often pulling together enough money to watch Hubbell pitch for the Giants at the Polo Grounds. He tried to imitate Hubbell, but their styles were just the opposite. He did, however, copy the way Hubbell laid his glove down—players left their gloves on the field in those days—and the way he avoided stepping on the baseline when he crossed it.

Hubbell had pinpoint control and a roundhouse curve, while

Vander Meer reared back and threw the ball as hard as he could, often with a wild streak. It wasn't until 1940 that Vander Meer got to pitch against Hubbell.

At age fifteen Johnny joined the Midland Rangers, named after the New York Rangers hockey team. During one game the Rangers were without a pitcher, so Johnny volunteered to take the mound. For pitching semipro ball he received thirty cents an inning, a welcome sum during the height of the Great Depression.

"I was wild as a hawk at first," he said. "In my first game I don't know how many players I hit, but I walked at least ten in three innings. I did not give up many hits. I walked too many to let them hit me."

They probably were too frightened to stay in the batter's box long enough to swing the bat. Johnny's wildness carried over into his Major League years, proving to be something he could never shake.

The Rangers rarely lost when the left-hander was on the mound. His blazing fastball and his wildness intimidated batters. When it started to get dark, batters would stand as far as four feet from the plate and swing wildly at the first three pitches no matter where they went, just happy to strike out and return to the dugout without getting plunked—or, if they were brave enough, to stick around long enough to draw a walk.

Johnny's parents, who were active in the Christian Reformed Church, took a jaundiced view of their son's baseball activities. They called the game a "loafer's paradise." "It was a ticklish situation with them," he said. "When they saw how much I wanted to play, they were willing to let me go." But they wouldn't let him play ball on Sundays because it was the Sabbath, forcing him to turn down more money for pitching on Sunday afternoons than he would have made all week.

His father wanted young Johnny to join him in the mill along with his brothers. "The mill was everything to him," Vander Meer said. "He thought the mill couldn't operate without him."

But Johnny loved the outdoors. "I'd have been a game warden before I'd have done that."

When he signed his first baseball contract he used a little rationalization that would allow him to play on Sundays. "I felt . . . if anyone had outstanding talent in a trade, that was good, and it was a sin not to use it."

Johnny's friends and relatives at the June 15 game weren't surprised by his pitching prowess. He had pitched a number of no-hitters in sandlot ball in northern New Jersey. He remembered those days so fondly that when it became evident he would never make the Hall of Fame, he gave his memorabilia to Midland Park for display in the Veterans Memorial Library.

On dedication day at the library, Vander Meer, then eighty-two years old, remembered his days playing ball in the tiny town. "I guess the good old days of the Rangers and the Midland Park [Athletic Club] series was probably a bigger thrill for me then than a couple World Series I was able to take care of and get involved in," he said. "And I'll never forget it, because you folks here in [Midland] Park gave me as a kid the ambition and a real desire to want to become a big leaguer."

In 1932 Johnny pitched five no-hit, no-run games and finished the year 14-1. His loss came at the hands of the barnstorming Israelite House of David team, a religious group that featured bearded players from Benton Harbor, Michigan, who preached to potential members along the way. They rarely lost a game.

For three straight years the Rangers beat the Midland Park Athletic Club, a team of grown men, in a three-game series to determine the town champions. "We had as many people come to those games as there were in the community [of] 2,500 to 3,000," Vander Meer said.

Johnny set his sights set on a professional baseball career not only because he loved the game but also because a young man who was a high school dropout had no other career options besides working in the mill his entire life. Baseball was his out.

"When I played players had more desire," Vander Meer said in 1983. "We were Depression players. There weren't any jobs, and baseball was the only vehicle. Where else was there any money?"

Writing about baseball during the Depression, author Charles C. Alexander explained, "The times were tough for just about everybody, including the young men who tried to make their way as professional baseball players in a decade of persistently discouraging prospects in most kinds of employment."

Johnny soon was going to get the break he had hoped for.

Second Inning 5

Center fielder Harry Craft led off for the Reds in the second inning. Craft, twenty-three, was a decent hitter (.263) but stood out defensively. He was a smooth, smart outfielder who helped train, among others, Mickey Mantle in defensive skills during his sixty years as a player, scout, coach, and manager. During the 1938 season Craft hit .270 with fifteen homers and eighty-three RBIs, his best season in his six-year career. As a fielder he made just 8 errors in 459 chances.

Craft's defense put him at the top that season, but he is probably best known for hastening the advent of foul-pole screens with a disputed home run at the Polo Grounds in 1939. Craft flied out deep to left fielder Hassett.

Up next was the left-handed, twenty-eight-year-old third baseman Lew Riggs. Riggs was little more than an average player in his ten-year career, most of it spent as a part-timer except for four years with the Reds from 1935 to 1938. Riggs made twenty-four defensive errors in 1938. He was hitting .242 when he stepped to the plate to hit against Butcher. Riggs also flied out to Hassett.

Then Billy Myers, another light-hitting infielder, stepped up to the plate with a .240 batting average. He also was an erratic fielder, compiling 31 errors in 676 chances. His six-year career was dampened by personal matters that at least once kept him off the field for an extended period. Myers flied out to Koy.

In the bottom half of the second inning the Dodgers sent up their best hitter, catcher Ernest Gordon "Babe" Phelps, also nicknamed "Blimp" because of his six-foot-two-inch, 225-pound frame. Later, after he refused to fly on airplanes, his nickname was amended to "The Grounded Blimp."

Phelps might have been considered the biggest catcher in the Major Leagues were it not for Ernie Lombardi, his opposing catcher that day. Thirty-year-old Phelps was born in Odenton, Maryland, one of ten children. He was called Babe not only because he bore a resemblance to Babe Ruth but also because he had a swing similar to the Bambino's.

Phelps was a colorful character. The Dodgers once lost a close one in the ninth inning after Phelps called for knuckle-baller Dutch Leonard to throw a fastball. The resulting pitch was quickly knocked out of the park to end the game.

In the dugout, Stengel asked Phelps why he had called for a fastball. Phelps responded, "His knuckle ball is tough to catch!" The exasperated Stengel responded, "If his knuckler's tough to catch, don't you think it might be tough to hit, too?" Stengel's advice came too late to save his own job; 1936 was his last season as the Dodgers' skipper.

Phelps, another left-hander, was hitting .324. In 1936 he hit .367, a batting average no Major League catcher has surpassed since then. In 2009 Minnesota Twins catcher Joe Mauer came close, at .365.

Vander Meer coaxed Phelps to ground out to Frey for the first out of the second inning. Phelps went hitless in five at bats against Vandy in his career.

Next up was Harry Arthur "Cookie" Lavagetto, who was in a close race with Lombardi as the leading hitter in the National League. Lavagetto got his nickname from the owner of the Pacific Coast League's Oakland Oaks, his first professional team. His Oakland teammates called him "Cookie's boy" because he had been hired by the Oaks' president, Victor "Cookie" Devincenzi.

"Cookie was a character," said a newspaperman who covered the Dodgers. "He walked funny and always needed a shave. His shirt would be hanging out of his pants, and he wore his hat at a weird angle. Cookie would just sit there, not realizing he looked any different than the next guy."

"Oh, I used to know it," Lavagetto said. "I used to enjoy wearing one sock up, the other down. I don't know why exactly. I just enjoyed it." Lavagetto was a good two-strike hitter, especially with men on base. He played ten years in the Majors, his first three with Pittsburgh, the remainder with Brooklyn. He finished his career with a .269 batting average. His best year was 1939, when he hit .300. Later he managed the Washington Senators for four years and then became the first manager of the Minnesota Twins.

Vander Meer got Lavagetto to hit a ground ball to Myers, who threw him out. Lavagetto had no luck hitting against Vandy in his entire career, going 0 for 18, although he did draw six walks.

Next up for Vandy was free-swinging first baseman Dolph Camilli, who was batting .268. Camilli had hit at least twenty-three home runs in eight straight seasons. He had been traded to the Dodgers in March after playing for the Cubs and the Phillies.

Camilli led the league in walks that year with 119, but he struck out 101 times, the second-worst record in the league. This happened despite Camilli's superstition, according to Leo Durocher, that "it was good luck to rub the batboy's head before going to the plate."

Standing five feet ten inches tall, Camilli, thirty-one, had a muscular physique and soft hands. No one ever challenged him to a fight. Said Durocher, "Nobody knew how well Dolph could fight because, quite frankly, nobody had ever wanted to find out." Durocher commented that Camilli was "a quiet, gentle man, but he was strong as an ox."

In a 1976 article in *Esquire* magazine, sportswriter Harry Stein published an "All Time All-Star Argument Starter" that consisted of five ethnic baseball teams. Camilli was the first baseman on Stein's Italian team.

Camilli, who was 2 for 17 in his career against Vandy, also had little luck that day. Vander Meer walked him, making Camilli the first to get on base for the Dodgers in the game.

The Chief, center fielder Ernie Koy, came up next. Koy got his nickname because he was part Native American. In those days, virtually all players with Indian heritage were called by the common, racist moniker Chief.

Koy made his debut in the Majors that year with the Dodgers. The twenty-eight-year-old rookie had blazing speed. He'd been a football and baseball star for the Texas Longhorns and a three-time All-Southwest Conference selection for football.

Koy left the University of Texas in 1934 and graduated from Sam Houston State Teachers College in 1938. He then chose baseball over pro football, which was still in its formative stages. After getting traded from the Yankees to the Dodgers, Koy played more games in 1938, his first year in the Majors, than any other season in his five-year career. He later spent time with the Cardinals, Phillies, and Reds, appearing in a total of 558 games. Koy never returned to baseball after serving in the navy in World War II. He was as successful as any Dodger batting against Vander Meer, going 5 for 14 during his career. Koy was batting .312 when he stepped to the plate and promptly popped out to Frey.

Third Inning **6**

Here was Vandy pitching against the Dodgers, a team he could have been toiling for. Brooklyn gave the left-hander a boost toward a Major League career while he was still a teenager.

Vander Meer first caught the interest of a northern New Jersey baseball fan, an oil salesman named Fred Pridmore, for his pitching in the Midland Park sandlot games. Pridmore arranged a tryout for Johnny with the Giants. Vandy worked out at the Giants' ballpark, the Polo Grounds, but he failed to attract much attention. Later that day he watched a game between the Giants and the St. Louis Cardinals before returning home. He never heard another word from the New York team.

Then Vandy got a second chance. He was selected to appear in a documentary produced by the National League, aimed at drumming up young men's interest in a baseball career. A scout who had seen him pitch a sandlot no-hitter recommended him. Dodgers business manager Dave Driscoll had been put in charge of finding a "typical American boy" to star in the film.

A representative of the National League's president, John A. Heydler, told Driscoll, "What I really want is a boy from a modest home, one whose father is of moderate means, and principally a kid who has some chance of sticking with the club. The movie will promote baseball, and it will show the average American kid that he, too, may have such a chance."

"I've got the very boy for you," Driscoll replied, "one who answers every requirement you have set up." He put forth Vander Meer, whom the Dodgers had been scouting and planned to offer a tryout. Vandy was the perfect candidate for leading man—

tall, well-built at 175 pounds, and handsome. He had bushy eyebrows, a firm, well-chiseled chin, a smile good enough for a toothpaste ad, good color, plenty of blond hair on his chest, a soft voice, and a slow-speaking manner. He dressed neatly in gabardine summer suits with striped ties, seldom swore, and didn't drink. Driscoll recommended Vander Meer even though he wasn't convinced Vandy had the talent to play for the Dodgers. "He looked like someone made to order for the part of America's most promising novice."

Johnny couldn't wait to head to Florida for the tryout. Before he left, the film crew shot him with his parents, packing for the trip, and then catching the train for the Dodgers' spring training camp in Coral Gables. Once there, the film crew took motion pictures of him eating, meeting with the coaches and players, and enjoying his time off the field. The movie was shown as part of the Movietone News at Saturday matinees in theaters across the country. As for Johnny's performance, Al Lopez, who later managed the Cleveland Indians and Chicago White Sox and earned a spot in the Hall of Fame, remembered that the left-hander was so wild only two Dodgers would take batting practice—Hack Wilson, a future Hall of Famer, and Lefty O'Doul, a hard-hitting left-hander.

"I'll never forget Lefty O'Doul, who was a real pal to me in that training camp," Vander Meer recalled. "I don't think I missed hitting a single spot on his body, but he stood up there and kept taking his cuts. 'Keep firing, kid,' he'd yell out to me. That was real encouragement." One observer said that the way Vander Meer threw at O'Doul gave new meaning to the word *dodger*.

"Any boy in America could have the opportunity to play in the big leagues," Vander Meer said years later. "Of course, it was a one in ten thousand shot if you broke into the game and played ten years. That's what the odds were at that time."

But those odds didn't stop Johnny from chasing his rainbow. "I tried so hard I pretended every pitch was a third strike to Babe Ruth," he said.

Dodgers manager Max Carey was not impressed. Johnny was about to be sent home when Joe Shaute, a veteran pitcher and also a left-hander, suggested that Carey give Vander Meer a second chance and not release him. Carey laughed and said, "We can't release him because we never signed him. He was just down here on some silly movie."

Shaute had taken a shine to "the kid with the funny name" and gave him some tips. "I'll always be grateful to Joe," Vander Meer recalled several years later. "His friendly help, not only then but later also, proved a turning point in my career."

Carey relented. He sent Vander Meer to the Dayton Ducks in the Class C Middle Atlantic League under the tutelage of Ducky Holmes for $125 a month. "I had been making more than that playing semi-pro ball," Vander Meer said. He could barely make ends meet, but he wasn't discouraged. He loved baseball. "If someone had offered me a job at twice my salary doing something else I would have refused it."

Now Vander Meer was pitching against those very same Dodgers in Ebbets Field under the lights—and not far from his hometown. The Reds gave Vander Meer all the runs he needed in the third inning, all of which came after two were out. Vander Meer, a good hitter for a pitcher (.241), led off the inning and bounced back to Butcher. Then Frey popped out to Camilli. Wally Berger beat out an infield hit to third and took second on Lavagetto's wild throw to first. Butcher walked Goodman, which brought up big Frank McCormick, who hit Butcher's first pitch for a three-run homer over the left-field fence. The blast was just his second home run of the season. The Reds picked up another run when Lombardi walked. Craft and Riggs followed with singles, running the score to 4–0. The Dodgers brought in reliever Tot Pressnell, who got Myers looking at a third strike.

Leo Durocher, the scrappy Dodgers shortstop, led off the bottom of the third inning. Durocher, nicknamed "The Lip" for his outspoken manner, was known for his competitiveness, passion, ego, and knack for remembering situations. "Show me a good loser," he said, "and I'll show you an idiot." He had come to the Dodgers in a trade on October 14, 1937, at the end of his playing career, but the idea was for him to take over managing the Dodgers, which he did the next year. His twenty-six-year managerial career led to his election to the Hall of Fame in 1994.

Durocher managed nine years with the Dodgers, eight with the Giants, seven with the Cubs, and two with the Astros. He played seventeen years in the field, including the last five as player-manager for the Dodgers. He also played for the Yankees, the Reds, and the Cardinals before coming to Brooklyn. He was a lifetime .247 hitter, although he could be dangerous in the clutch. In the field he possessed only average ability with the glove.

Durocher, who was batting .254, never had much luck against Vandy, managing one hit in fifteen at bats against him.

The left-hander got Durocher to bounce back to the mound. That brought up knuckleball pitcher Forest Charles Pressnell, more commonly known as Tot, who had relieved Butcher with two outs in the top of the third. Pressnell got his nickname from being the last of eight children. His brothers were much older, and the "Tot" used to tag along with them.

Pressnell toiled eight years in the Minors before being called up on April 21, 1938, compiling a 4-5 record with a respectable 2.98 ERA. As a pitcher he wasn't expected to be much of a hitter. He had nine hits the entire year while appearing in forty-three games. Pressnell struck out.

The Dodgers were back at the top of the order with Kiki Cuyler at bat for the second time. He drew Vander Meer's second walk. The next batter, Coscarart, hit a long fly that Berger ran down.

Reds general manager Warren Giles, who was in the stands, said after the catch, "It was then I said to myself, 'Well, maybe he's destined to do something nobody else has ever done.'"

So how were the Reds and Dodgers affected by playing at night? Although it was the first night game at Ebbets Field, it wasn't the first time they had played after dark. Several players had taken the field in night games in Cincinnati. If anything, the new, more powerful lights at Ebbets Field were better than at Crosley Field.

Catcher Phelps recalled years later that the impressive fireworks display preceding the game had left a "mist" in the air that affected visibility. But most players registered few complaints.

Brooklyn Eagle writer Tommy Holmes, who also wrote for the *Sporting News*, said the lights had no effect. "Everybody could follow the ball," he wrote. "That is, everybody except for the Dodgers, but that was entirely due to young Mr. Vander Meer and not any fault of the lighting."

The fact that one team banged out eleven hits and the other team none shows that the lights were a very small factor in the game's outcome, at least as far as the Reds were concerned. The Reds, of course, were more used to playing games under the lights. Perhaps more telling is that the Dodgers that year hit only .193 in their eight night games. Then again, the National League that season hit nearly thirty points lower in night games. Surely, then, lighting played some role, however small.

It is difficult to ignore the fact that during the four night games Vander Meer pitched, he had a 3-1 record with a credible 1.95 earned run average, while he was 12-9 with a 3.35 ERA in day games during the 1938 season.

Another factor was Brooklyn's inability to hit well against

Vander Meer in daytime or at night. The Dodgers faced Vandy in twenty-five innings over four games and managed nine hits. He walked eighteen, however, which helped lead to his 2.52 ERA against the Dodgers.

Certainly lighting wasn't as good as in today's parks, which can seem like daylight. Ebbets Field was illuminated with 615 incandescent bulbs that each generated fifteen hundred watts. Compare that with today's Chase Field, home of the Arizona Diamondbacks, with 708 metal halide (high-intensity discharge) lamps generating fifteen hundred watts apiece. Also, because Chase Field is mostly indoors—it has a retractable roof—the park tends to hold in light rather than allowing it to escape into the night. It is noteworthy that new parks such as those in Minneapolis and San Francisco are using LEED lighting, which helps keep light from leaking out into nearby neighborhoods and is more energy efficient as well.

The first night game in Crosley Field in 1935 created considerable controversy about playing under the lights. In that May 24 game the Reds beat the Phillies 2–1 behind Paul Derringer. "There were few hard-hit balls in the game," the *Literary Digest* noted. "The batters gave the impression of not taking toe-holds at the plate for fear of being hit with a pitched ball."

The Reds' Sammy Byrd, for one, didn't care for the lights. He crashed into the center-field wall chasing a hit and crumpled to the ground. "The lighting was poor so I couldn't see the wall, but one of the other fielders yelled that I had plenty of room so I went for the ball, hit the wall, hurt my knee and knocked myself out. My knee was never right after that. We all thought the game was a gimmick and none of us felt there would be a future in it."

Phillies player-manager Jimmie Wilson, later to become a Red, seemed resolved that night baseball was here to stay. "I wouldn't like to play it every night, but if it will make money, and there doesn't seem to be any doubt that it will, we'll have to play."

Umpires weren't wild about it, either. Bill Klem said more players swung at bad balls than in any game he had umped that year. "We had no trouble making calls in the infield, but it was difficult to see catches in the outfield."

A fine mist made visibility even worse, Klem said. It was impossible "to determine from home plate whether a long fly had been caught until the fielder drew back his arm to return the ball to the infield."

But a couple of years later veteran umpire Dolly Stark, who also was umpiring that night in Brooklyn, had some good words about nighttime baseball, particularly regarding the weather. "I've never yet seen a night game that was half as bad, from the weather standpoint, as most daytime games in April. In July and August it's a lot more comfortable at night than in the afternoon."

Pitcher Joe Bowman said he suspected most of the players had at one time or another played night baseball but under poor lights. Reds second baseman Lonny Frey played under bad lighting in the Minors. "I remember three popups above home plate in Baltimore one night that got above the level of the lights. None of them were caught. One almost hit the catcher in the head. The other thing I remember is that when the lights were first put up [in the Minors] and it rained and the lights got wet, pow! They'd blow up."

Even Eastern sportswriters got into the act, calling Cincinnati a "hick town" for using lights. But Vander Meer had no problems with the lights. He had played dozens of games in the Minors under the lights, and the lighting in Crosley Field was much better. "There weren't any shadows," he recalled. "Actually you can see the ball better at night than in the daytime . . . because you never take your eye off of it at night."

But in Ebbets Field that historic night Vander Meer didn't see the ball too well, as he struck out against Pressnell to lead off the fourth inning.

He then coaxed Frey into hitting a slow grounder that Durocher charged and threw him out. The next batter, Berger, lined a double over shortstop into the gap, but Pressnell got Goodman to ground to Coscarart, who got him easily at first.

As the Reds took the field in the bottom of the fourth, a buzz began to run through the crowd. Usually fans aren't thinking of no-hitters until after the fifth inning, but this was different. Vandy hadn't given up a hit in twelve straight innings. It is unlikely anyone in Ebbets was unaware that the Dodgers had no hits.

In the bottom half of the fourth, Hassett grounded to McCormick, who lobbed to Vander Meer covering first base for the first out.

In the field, Vandy was decent with the glove. He made twenty-nine errors over thirteen years in 346 appearances on the mound. McCormick also was an excellent fielder, making only seven errors that year in 1,543 chances. In his career McCormick committed only seventy-eight errors in 14,877 chances.

Vander Meer then fanned Phelps, his third strikeout of the night, and got Lavagetto to fly out to Goodman.

Fifth Inning **8**

In the fifth the Reds again went quietly. McCormick was thrown out by Lavagetto on a close play. Lombardi grounded out to Durocher. Craft singled but was thrown out trying to stretch it to a double, Hassett to Coscarart.

Lombardi's groundout to Durocher lends itself to a story The Lip told three years later, when he was the Dodgers' player-manager and considering retirement. Lombardi had smacked a ground ball to Durocher. "The ball came to me on a perfect hop," Durocher said, "and I made a perfect throw to first base—but Lombardi beat it by a full step. In the clubhouse after the game, I said to the players: 'Get the scissors and cut the uniform off me. When I can't throw Lombardi out on a play like that, I've got to quit.' And that's what I did."

In the bottom of the fifth Camilli came up for the third time and bounced back to Vander Meer, who tossed to McCormick for the out.

The Brooklyn fans were beginning to cheer for Vandy as he mowed down Dodger after Dodger, chanting, one, two, three, four, strike. "Brooklyn fans were probably the most loyal fans in baseball, but when they saw what was going on, they pulled for me," he said.

Among the fans was Vander Meer's longtime friend Dick Jeffer. "[The fans] knew we were from Midland Park, and they were [yelling] 'you're gonna get beat,' and they were all hopped up because of the first night game, but the tune changed . . . when they started to root for Vander Meer because they realized what they were seeing would be a part of history." In the Ebbets Field press box "even hard-boiled sportswriters screamed, 'Come on Kid,'" wrote a *Time* reporter.

Back in Cincinnati, fans had no idea that history was in the making. They heard half-hour bulletins that gave the score after a certain inning, but the details were left to the morning newspapers.

Vandy said he knew he had a chance for a no-hitter in the fourth inning, even though Brooklyn fans made him aware of it from the first inning. "Of course, I didn't have it in my hip pocket," he said, "but I felt mighty good and my arm was ok."

In keeping with baseball tradition, none of his teammates mentioned the no-hitter. His teammates moved away from him. "Nobody on the bench said a word to me. Didn't want to put the whammie on me, I guess."

If it's true that pitching the first no-hitter takes its emotional toll on a pitcher, someone forgot to tell Vander Meer. He kept cruising along.

Koy followed Camilli, trying to bunt his way on, but Vandy threw him out. Koy must not have heard of the unwritten baseball rule that you don't try to break up a no-hitter by bunting.

Durocher closed out the inning by fouling out to Lombardi.

In 1933 Vandy was still struggling to find his way in baseball, and that season with the Dayton Ducks in the Mid-Atlantic League was one to remember. He suffered financially, playing for an eccentric owner-manager his straight-laced mother surely would not have appreciated. On the other hand, Vandy was having the time of his life doing what he wanted to do—play baseball.

He considered himself lucky when he got half of his $125 a month salary. "When payday came around they'd say, 'How much do you need to get by?' . . . At the end of the season they owed me $250. Everybody was at the bottom of the barrel in those days."

Owner-manager Howard "Ducky" Holmes shorted all of his

players. "He did it to me and to all of the other guys," Vander Meer said, claiming that Holmes owed "everybody" money.

Even if they weren't being shorted, Minor League players had a difficult time getting by financially. Most of them worked in the off-season. Vandy worked for as little as fifty cents an hour as a mason or plumber. "I had to," he said. "I was never in debt in my life. I didn't have any money and I didn't have any way to get into debt. The minor leagues back then were rough. But that was what we wanted to do, what we ate, what we slept, and what we drank. We had that desire to stay hungry in order to accomplish what we wanted."

Holmes was a former ballplayer and American League umpire who was dubbed Ducky because of his particularly long beak, or nose. "If my mother had known Ducky Holmes, I guarantee that I would have been home in fifteen minutes," Vander Meer recalled. "He'd do things like get drunk and get kicked out of the ballpark. He'd leave and go find a light pole to climb outside of the park. When he'd get up there he'd have a bottle in his back pocket and he'd give us signs from up on the light pole. Then after the game, the city would have to come with a ladder and take him down."

One umpire, Dan Tehan, who had his run-ins with Holmes, said that when Ducky would bring his batting order to home plate at the start of the game he would be sober. "Later when he came storming out to argue his breath might blow you off. We never figured out where he had the stuff hidden in the dugout."

On one occasion, Vander Meer said, a Dayton player, Pants Powell, tagged up on third base on a play to win the ball game on a fly ball. "Pants could really fly. He slid home and just beat the throw. Ducky took off from the coaching line and slid right behind him, stuck his spike in [Powell's] back, and they had to put about eighteen stitches in Pants' back."

During another game Ducky pedaled around the bases on a bicycle. "He made an amateur out of Bill Veeck," Vander Meer said.

Life in the Minor Leagues was no summer camp for boys. They rode from town to town in antiquated buses that couldn't top thirty-five miles per hour, stayed in fleabag hotels, and sometimes camped in parks without locker rooms or showers. They received $1.50 a day for meals. "That was only when you were on the road," Vander Meer said. "And if you left after twelve o'clock noon to go on a trip, like to Zanesville, you only got fifty cents."

When he played in the Mid-Atlantic League the players called it the Mad Atlantic because of the rigors of travel. "Like Branch Rickey used to say all the time, they kept us lean and hungry," Vander Meer said.

In Vandy's first year he had eleven wins and ten losses with an earned run average of 4.28. In 183 innings, he struck out 132 and walked 74.

Holmes apparently didn't think Vandy had much of a career ahead of him. He refused to recommend the left-hander to Major League teams interested in buying his contract.

Vander Meer could have been pitching for Brooklyn instead of Cincinnati had the Dodgers not listened to Ducky Holmes. The Dodgers held first rights to any ballplayer that Holmes owned. Bob Quinn, the Dodgers' business manager, and team manager Casey Stengel visited Dayton in 1933 to check out prospects. Holmes said he had none.

"Don't take that guy," Holmes said, pointing toward Vander Meer. "He'll never be a pitcher." Then he pointed toward a big first baseman and said, "And don't waste any time on that guy. He'll never hit." That player was Frank McCormick, later to become Vandy's teammate on the Reds, an eight-time All-Star and the National League's Most Valuable Player in 1941. The Dodgers listened to the advice and passed on both.

When Vander Meer wouldn't sign a new contract until he got his back pay, Holmes shipped him off to the Albany Senators in the then–Double A International League. Vander Meer never played with the Albany team, as he still wanted to play for Dayton. But, again, he wouldn't sign, and he was sold to the Scranton Miners in the Class A New York–Penn League. The Miners had a working relationship with the Boston Bees. Vandy was paid just $150 a month, but at least he received all his pay.

Apparently Holmes didn't have the consent of the Dodgers when he shipped Vander Meer to Scranton, where he brought a lot more money than if had stayed in the Dodgers' system.

When Vander Meer arrived in Scranton, manager Jake Pitler knew little about him and had him throw batting practice for two weeks before giving him a start. Vandy won his first two games. He ended the season with eleven wins, eight losses, and an earned run average of 3.73 in 164 innings. He won one game 2–1 despite walking sixteen batters.

At Scranton Vandy also worked hard on his fielding. He had lost several games thanks to his poor fielding. He'd pick up bunts or grounds and throw them into the grandstand or outfield. A Dayton sportswriter said outfielders and fans were in danger when Vander Meer got a fielding chance.

Vandy was injured shagging flies in the outfield at Scranton when his spike caught in the soggy turf and he landed on his left shoulder. He was out for two weeks. He blamed that injury for delaying his promotion to the Major Leagues.

During the off-season, Brooklyn general manager Bob Quinn argued that Vander Meer was the Dodgers' property and that his sale by Dayton to Scranton was illegal. The Dodgers appealed the sale to baseball commissioner Kenesaw Mountain Landis. But Landis upheld the sale, ruling that the Dodgers had lost interest in Vander Meer until he began showing signs of becoming a better pitcher after his season at Scranton.

Vandy returned to Scranton for the 1935 season, where he received a $50 pay raise to $200 a month. To his good fortune, he was reunited with Joe Shaute, who was finishing his career with the Miners. Shaute helped Vandy develop a change-up to go with his fastball and curve.

A sore arm that he picked up in the first game of the season hampered Vander Meer that entire season, and he wound up with seven wins and ten losses with a 5.35 ERA. He threw eighty-eight strikeouts while walking ninety in 133 innings.

All was not lost, however. Vander Meer had met a comely young woman, Lois, who lived across the street from the team's owner. While attending Scranton games she showed an interest in Vandy and asked one of his teammates to introduce them. She liked his quiet, unassuming ways, not to mention his blond, curly hair and dimples.

After fifty years of marriage, Lois Vander Meer said Vandy hadn't changed. Did he still have the dimples? a reporter asked her. "Certainly," she replied with a slight laugh, "but he may not have all of that curly hair."

Again Vander Meer was on the move. The Reds assigned him to the Durham Bulls, one of Cincinnati's Minor League properties. After the season Vandy was traded to Nashville. He decided he needed to see a doctor about his sore arm, which cost him the $300 he had managed to save.

His arm still bothered him, so he asked Nashville manager Jimmy Hamilton for help in getting his arm treated. Hamilton referred him to Lee Jensen, a doctor in Chattanooga, who told him that his problem was a muscle behind his shoulder. Jensen said he could fix Vander Meer's shoulder within ten days. "I was somewhat disappointed at his hasty diagnosis and complete confidence in my immediate recovery," Vandy said.

But with nothing to lose, Vander Meer underwent the treatments. After his ninth one, Dr. Jensen told him, "Johnny, you don't need treatment number ten. But I'm going to give it to you for luck. After it's over, you go to spring training and cut loose all you want." It worked, and Vander Meer reported to spring training.

In his first twenty-two innings at Nashville he gave up twenty-two runs and twenty-five walks. In his first start he walked the first three men he faced. "Didn't get a strike over. I had a 3-and-0 count on the fourth hitter and then, glory be, I got a strike over.

Know what happened? The Nashville manager lifted me. I still think I'm the only pitcher ever taken out of a ball game after throwing a strike."

Nashville offered him to the Red Sox for $25,000, but they turned down the offer. "Your price is out of the question," Sox business manager Billy Evans told Nashville's president, Fay Murray. "No player out of Class B baseball ever sold before for more than $7,500."

Murray replied, "This boy is an exception. He's going to be a star in the majors." Murray then offered Vander Meer to MacPhail, who countered with a bid for $17,500 and a player, which Nashville accepted. He was assigned to Durham, the Reds' new farm team in the Piedmont League.

Vandy's arm started to get stronger. The next time he started he struck out nineteen batters, breaking a league record. During his next two starts he fanned fifteen and seventeen and then broke his own record, striking out twenty.

In the league playoffs, Vander Meer struck out thirty more in two games that he won. He wound up fanning 295 batters in 214 innings during the season. But he was still plagued with wildness, walking 116 batters. He wound up winning nineteen games and losing six. It earned him the *Sporting News* Minor League Player of the Year Award. The *News* said his speed on his fastball "makes it appear as though they're hummingbird's eggs."

Years later, Vander Meer compared himself with Dodgers great Sandy Koufax. "We were both hard-throwing, no-control lefthanders when we came up. My wildness was uncontrollable. There were times when I didn't know where the hell the ball was going. But if I was on my game that night, I could be pretty damned hard to hit."

At Durham Johnny Gooch, who was the catcher as well as manager, noted that Vandy didn't pitch well with men on first base. He'd look nervously in that direction and then throw wild to home plate. In one game Vander Meer gave up a single in the ninth inning of a one-run game. Gooch called for a pitchout and then let the ball get by him. The runner moved over to third base. Gooch trotted out to the mound, handed Vandy the ball, and said, "Well, there's nobody on first base to bother you now. Do your stuff." Vander Meer proceeded to strike out the next three batters to win the game.

Gooch also helped him in another manner. Vander Meer had trouble hitting the outside corner of the plate. Gooch had an idea. "What if we moved the plate a little bit outside?" the manager said. So they did. That night Gooch, Vandy, and the groundskeeper went to the ballpark, pried up home plate, and moved it two inches toward first base, since most of the hitters Vander Meer would face the next day were right-handed hitters.

"Nobody knew the difference except us," Vander Meer said later. "Sure enough, my low and outside pitches began to get the corner of the plate for a strike."

When Vandy wasn't pitching, they moved the plate back to its original spot. "After dark it was easy to put the plate back where it belonged for the other pitchers," he said.

That story has the ring of myth more than fact. Moving home plate would have affected the baseline alignment with the plate. Surely an opposing manager or player or an umpire would have noticed.

Gooch said it was often difficult to catch Vander Meer. "I can't think of anyone as fast as he is," he said. "Catching him you have to have your mitt set one way, and you don't have time to shift it when he lets go of the ball."

During the winter Vander Meer returned home to Midland Park, where he worked as a stonemason for twenty-three dollars a week.

The Reds liked what they had seen of Vandy's previous season and invited him to their spring training camp in Florida in February 1937. Newspapers already were touting his skills. Read one newspaper headline, "Johnny Vander Meer May Cause Fans to Forget about Bob Feller in '37."

A news release prepared by the National League Service Bureau that spring called Vander Meer "a great young southpaw because he has one of the most effective fast balls in all baseball, regardless of league. He has the physical requisites necessary for speed and stamina, and apparently he has the heart to back up all these assets."

But the Reds weren't too sure that Vandy would make it in the big leagues. Business Manager Warren Giles debated whether he would pay the $7,500 still owed Nashville for Vandy. If he released the left-hander he wouldn't owe the money.

Vander Meer's showing in spring training failed to impress the club. He still was wild. Giles had to pay the money by April 15. "I didn't make up my mind [to keep him] until the last minute," Giles said.

It was the right decision. After Vander Meer's double no-hitters Giles estimated the pitcher was worth half a million dollars. "Anyway, I wouldn't take any price for him. He is priceless."

During spring training Vandy kept hearing from catcher Ernie Lombardi that he was counting the days until he could see his "old friend Mr. Hudie."

"Naturally, I'm curious," Vandy said. "'What makes this guy so special with Ernie,' I'm asking myself." He found out soon enough. As the Reds' train crossed the Ohio River into Cincinnati, Lombardi threw one of his huge arms around Vander Meer's shoulders and said, "There's Mr. Hudie." Vandy looked up to see a large billboard advertising Hudepohl beer. Its slogan was "Get moody with Hudie." The beer sign was one of many that decorated the outfield wall or poked up over the fences so they could be seen from the stands in Crosley Field.

9 A Dream Come True

Vandy called getting to the Major Leagues his biggest thrill in baseball. The big leagues didn't intimidate him. "When I walked into the Cincinnati clubhouse, I wasn't scared because I'd been around for a couple of years, and a clubhouse is a clubhouse, it's your work."

Vandy admired his locker and felt the flannel of the new uniform with his name on it. He would be making $3,500 a year now. Backup infielder Eddie Joost, Frank McCormick, Harry Craft, and backup catcher Willard Hershberger sat near his locker. "I realized a boy's dream. If I had to pick an individual thrill [in baseball], that was it," Vandy said.

But he had to work to keep that dream. "My toughest thing to do once I got my locker was to keep it," he said. "Somebody was trying to take it away from me for fifteen years." On another occasion he said, "It didn't take much to get you out of the big leagues. If things didn't go your way or you had injuries or you got cuffed around a little bit, they sent you out pretty quick."

Vander Meer knew what he was talking about; shortly after moving up to the Majors, it happened to him.

In his first start in the Major Leagues, on May 20, 1937, Vander Meer pitched a complete game but lost 3–1 to the Boston Bees. He gave up five hits, struck out eleven, and walked five.

Toward the middle of the year, the usually mild-mannered Vander Meer got into a row with Charlie Dressen, the five-foot-five, 146-pound manager, after a bad outing. After Vandy walked three straight batters in a game against Pittsburgh, Dressen strolled to the mound and told him, "I know what's wrong with you. You have no guts." Dressen sent him to the showers.

After the game, the six-foot-one, 195-pound Vander Meer loomed over Dressen. "If you don't think I have any guts, why don't you take a swing at me. I don't think you have the guts enough to do that."

Coach George "High Pockets" Kelly stepped between the two, and Dressen left the locker room. The next morning Vander Meer went to see General Manager Warren Giles, telling him that he had pitched his last game for the Reds and that he was leaving the club.

"I want out of here," he yelled at Giles. The general manager agreed to give him some time off.

Within a week Giles offered Vander Meer an assignment to Syracuse in the International League, which Vander Meer readily accepted. There he joined several future Reds players, including Frank McCormick and Harry Craft. It was just as well, for when a player got into Dressen's doghouse, he might not play again for a long while.

The *Sporting News* provided a little prophecy about Vandy's demotion. "Next year, perhaps, Vander Meer will be a wow for the Reds."

In a 1990 oral history on file with the Baseball Hall of Fame, Vander Meer said he asked to be sent to the Minors because he was not getting enough work, that when he pitched only once every ten days or so he lost some control.

"You can't lock a young horse in the barn on Monday and then take him out two weeks later and put him in the race," Vander Meer said.

Dressen got under Vandy's skin one other time, in 1951, when Dressen was managing the Dodgers and Vander Meer was with the Cubs. Vander Meer thought Dressen was stealing his signs, but Dressen said that was not true.

"He had a catcher who gave me the tip-off," Dressen said. "When Vandy was going to throw a curve the catcher would bring his knees back and forth several times. When it was a fast ball the catcher would move his knees together only once."

Vandy's record that abbreviated season in Cincinnati was 3-5 with an ERA of 3.84. He walked sixty-nine while striking out fifty-two. "Yes," he said the next season, "I guess I was an all-American flop that year."

He wasn't any better at Syracuse, still plagued by wildness. He had an auspicious start there, going in as a relief pitcher in the first game of a Labor Day doubleheader against the Baltimore Orioles. But he gave up a home run to the first batter he faced, which cost his team the game. In the second game he came in again and was hit hard, losing that game 4–0. He only gave up four hits in the seven-inning nightcap, but he walked four and gave up two home runs.

Vander Meer readily admitted that he was wild, but he defended himself by noting that his pitches just missed the strike zone. "I walked a lot of men, but I wasn't wild the way Bill Hallahan and Bob Feller and a few others are," he said. "It was very, very seldom that I had a wild pitch chalked against me or made the catcher stretch to snag a pitch."

Nobody moved home plate for him, and he wound up with five wins and eleven losses. His Minor League record to that point was 53-46. That winter Vander Meer decided not to work, spending his time hunting and ice fishing. He took time to tell Reds general manager Warren Giles that he wasn't giving up. "I know I'm a better ballplayer than the showing I made during the past season," he wrote in a letter to Giles.

Apparently Giles thought so, too. He told Vander Meer to join the Reds at training camp in Tampa in the spring of 1938. Because he hadn't played in many Major League games the previous year, Vandy was still considered a rookie.

He earned $500 a month, and Giles continued to pay Vander Meer that amount even while he was in the Minors. Vander Meer was extremely fond of Giles. He trusted him to be fair and to treat him right, so much so that he allowed Giles to handle his business affairs after he hurled his second no-hitter.

When Vandy arrived at spring training that year he wasn't even sure he was going to make the roster. He was glad to see that Giles had fired Dressen, and he found the new manager, Bill McKechnie, to his liking. Giles had won the battle with three other teams to lure McKechnie from the Bees.

"This fellow's the best manager in baseball," Giles said. "He'll bring a championship in two years at least. Maybe even this year."

Although Giles may have been looking at the team's long-term prospects, McKechnie was worried about the next game. He knew that managers were hired to be fired, calling it a game of heartbreaks for managers.

"You can't celebrate even a victory," he noted. "If you win today, you must start worrying about tomorrow. If you win a pennant, you start worrying about the World Series. As soon as that's over, you start worrying about next season."

Vandy found McKechnie accommodating, especially in light of his experience with Dressen. In turn, McKechnie had high hopes for Vander Meer.

McKechnie appreciated Vander Meer's work ethic, and Vander Meer liked the way McKechnie handled his players, particularly pitchers. He wasn't alone. Several pitchers over the years were heard to say, "If you can't pitch for McKechnie, you can't pitch for anybody."

McKechnie also liked Vandy's size. At six feet one inch and 195 pounds, Vander Meer was a carbon copy of the pitchers who had played for McKechnie. Teammate Paul Derringer was six foot three and 205 pounds, and Bucky Walters and Junior Thompson were the same size as Vander Meer. Whitey Moore was six one and 200 pounds, while Lee Grissom was six three and 200 pounds. All threw the ball hard.

But that wasn't good enough for McKechnie.

He worked with them to throw curve balls in crucial situations. "You're not a big league pitcher until you can throw a curve on command," he said. "I'm not going to get beat with my pitchers throwing fastballs."

McKechnie also refused to allow his pitchers to throw sliders, calling it "a sore-armed pitch."

Vander Meer said McKechnie liked to have his pitchers throw a curveball no matter what the count was on the batter. "And it was a very good philosophy because a curve ball is a lot harder to hit than a fastball."

The mild-mannered McKechnie also worked with pitchers on their tempers. He would not allow a pitcher to remain in a game if he lost his temper. "If you're angry, you can't think, and if you can't think you can't pitch for me," he said.

Fortunately, he didn't have to work hard with the soft-spoken Vander Meer.

McKechnie tried to treat his players fairly. "There's no secret to having a bunch of ballplayers hustling for you. Just treat them the way you would like to be treated," he said. "When they make a mistake, tell 'em about it, but don't abuse 'em. When they do well, tell 'em about that, too. Remember they're not all alike, and judge every man the way he's entitled to be judged—as an individual."

As manager of the Boston Bees at the time they unloaded Vandy, McKechnie later recalled what a mistake that had been. "I'm not going to let anybody take that boy from me this time," he said.

One of the first pieces of advice McKechnie gave Vander Meer was to focus. "Always have an idea where you're throwing a ball," he said. "Even in a pepper game pick out a certain spot each time you throw a ball and try to hit that exact spot."

During the team's first full-time workout of the spring, McKechnie and longtime coach Hank Gowdy, a former catcher, kept a close eye on Vandy.

"Look, Hank," McKechnie once said, pointing at Vander Meer. "The kid's control is all right when he throws overhand. When he slips into a half sidearm delivery, he loses control, and his ball goes high and wide." McKechnie knew that taming Vander Meer's wildness would turn the left-hander into a great pitcher. He needed to smooth out Vandy's pitching motion, in which he started by bending over and peering toward the plate while letting his arms dangle. Then he would pump both arms behind his back and swing them forward while almost dragging his glove and pitching hands on the ground. Next, he brought his hands back over his head and leaned back while kicking his right leg high in the air. Twisting forward, he then rifled the ball wildly to batters, who feared for their lives.

Vandy threw two pitches, a fastball and a curve. "I didn't even throw a changeup," he said.

He had a habit of frowning and looking skyward when a batter got a hit off him. If he walked a batter, he pounded his fist in his glove. As he left the mound, he avoided stepping on the baselines when he walked off the field; his only other superstition was placing his glove face up on the sidelines after an inning. (In those days players were allowed to leave their gloves on the field.) In the dugout he was quiet—not much rah-rah in him.

McKechnie changed Vander Meer's pitching motion from three-quarters sidearm to directly overhand to improve his follow-through. McKechnie felt confident that the changes would make Vander Meer a winner. "That kid has the makings of one of the greatest young pitchers in the game."

In working with Vandy, McKechnie explained his philosophy for coaching pitchers. "We don't try to make overhand pitchers out of sidearmers or vice versa," he said. "What Gowdy and I have tried to do in our long association is try to determine the best natural qualifications of any player, particularly pitchers, and then show them ways to improve on those qualifications."

When Vander Meer lapsed into old habits, he would hear McKechnie hollering from the bench, "Overhand, John, overhand."

McKechnie and Gowdy also noticed that Vandy threw wildest when he started his windup while erect and then twisted around, a move that impeded his follow-through. This may have been the first time in Vander Meer's career that he received such coaching. Most other teams just threw him into the fray and let him pitch.

McKechnie had Vander Meer bend over at the waist with his arms at his sides. Then, as he straightened up, he would pull his left arm back, rear back with his right leg high, and then throw straight ahead.

But Vandy still failed to properly follow through. One day that spring, during drills, Gowdy called Vander Meer over. "I've been talking to you and McKechnie has been talking to you," he grumbled. "Today I'm not going to talk to you. I'm going to let you look."

Gowdy pointed to future Hall of Fame pitcher Lefty Grove, a sometimes grumpy veteran who was warming up. "Watch him closely," Gowdy said. "See how he keeps the ball in front of him when he pitches."

Gowdy then suggested that McKechnie ask Grove to work with Vander Meer. Between 1930 and 1936 Grove had won 166 games pitching for the Athletics and the Red Sox. Sportswriter Arthur "Bugs" Baer once said about Grove, "He could throw a lamb chop past a wolf."

Who better to teach Vander Meer how to bring his wildness under control than Grove? "There never was a wilder man than Lefty Grove when he was with the Baltimore Orioles," a news release from the National League Service Bureau said.

Baseball statistician Bill James recalled one incident when Grove of the Minor League Baltimore Orioles pitched against Glenn Wright of the Kansas City Blues in the 1923 Junior World Series. Grove's first pitch sailed behind Wright's head. Years later Wright asked Grove if he remembered that pitch. "Sure," Grove said, "It went behind you, but I didn't mean it to." Wright replied, "If I had known that I'd have been even more scared."

Asking Grove to help Vandy was risky at best. Grove was quiet and grumpy. He just wanted to be left alone, so much so that he often became temperamental—ornery, even. Several sportswriters and players disliked him.

But Grove saw himself in the young left-hander, and he agreed to help. Grove told Vander Meer that he, too, had been wild in his early years, and he'd begun to pitch better only when he learned to follow through.

"He took me into the clubhouse," Vander Meer said, "and spent quite a while showing me just what he did to overcome his trouble."

"I was wild because I was letting the ball go too soon and not following through," Grove said. He instructed Vander Meer to follow through until his left arm struck his right knee. "Try to hold the ball as long as you possibly can," Grove told him. "Don't let go until the last second, and keep your eyes glued to the plate. [Vander Meer had been looking at the ground when releasing the ball.] If you'll bend your right knee instead of holding it stiff and then sweep down with your left arm until your elbow strikes the knee, I believe you'll get better results. Always let the ball go directly in front of your body."

Vandy never forgot the help Grove gave him. "I was getting a million dollars' worth of advice from one of the greatest southpaws in baseball, and getting it for nothing," he said.

When it appeared that Vander Meer had mastered the follow-through, McKechnie had him go into a rocking motion to generate more power and to lengthen his stride. Vandy bruised his left forearm with constant practice of the motion where his arm hit his leg. "But I achieved what I was after [when] I began holding the ball a fleeting instant longer, enough that I was looking directly at the plate when I threw it and I was getting it over."

McKechnie was patient with Vandy. He would watch him through his steel-rimmed glasses while thoughtfully stroking his chin. "I was able to concentrate exactly on what he told me," Vander Meer said. "I knew I didn't have to rush or be afraid if I took my time."

Vandy always referred to his manager as Mr. McKechnie. "I

can sincerely say that I was proud to play for [McKechnie]," Vander Meer said. "He was one of the greatest individuals I ever met in my life, either on the field or off. Ballplayers never feared McKechnie; they respected him."

McKechnie had a pronounced effect on Vander Meer's career. "Nobody thought I was good but Bill McKechnie . . . who told me, when I arrived at spring training in Florida, that he was counting on me to be a regular. He said he believed I could make it. He gave me hope"

Another time Vander Meer added, "I'll never forget the day that spring we were at Lynchburg, Virginia. I was pitching batting practice and after a little while McKechnie, on the bench, began to yell: 'He's got it! He's got it! That boy is going to make it.'"

As for Grove, when the Reds traveled with the Red Sox during spring training games on the way north, Vander Meer sat in the Red Sox bullpen and listened to the veteran pitcher's baseball wisdom. "He always had that great will to win and he helped fix that in my mind. I absorbed as much as I possibly could and became a real Lefty Grove fan.

"I'll never be able to thank Lefty [enough] for his friendliness and smartness in putting his fingers on my errors," Vander Meer said. "McKechnie kept giving me great advice, too, all spring."

Sixth Inning 10

Johnny felt lucky to play for McKechnie, for the fatherly Mc-Kechnie was a player's manager. He was a well-bred gentleman who was highly religious and knew how to handle his players. In turn they played hard for him. He was known as "The Deacon" because he was so religious. He had sung in his church choir for twenty-five years. He didn't cuss, drink, or raise his voice. "I've seen guys with ten times my ability who couldn't make it because they took a drink," he once said. "What a tragedy."

In his career McKechnie won four pennants with three different teams, two World Series title, and a manager-of-the-year award when his team finished in the second division. He was selected for the Hall of Fame in 1962. His secret? Field a fine defensive team and teach players to play better than they knew how.

He knew how to get the best out of his players. He praised those who needed it and reamed out those he thought would benefit from it. He was always proud of his teams and publicly defended each one. He saved his wrath for the umpires, who often wondered where all that nice guy stuff came from.

Leo Durocher once described how McKechnie approached an umpire when he disagreed with a call. "Out of the dugout walked . . . McKechnie. The way he always did, with his arms crossed and walking real slow as if it pained him deeply to have to be doing this," Durocher said. "He wore glasses, and he had a mild, reasonable way about him that allowed him to get away with murder. Every other manager I ever knew came running out there. Myself, I couldn't get there quick enough to get thrown out. I decided to do it McKechnie's way once, walking nice and easy, keeping my voice down, and I got thrown out, anyway."

Reds historian Lee Allen said, "There is an air about him that makes others want to appear at their best. He is the sort of man that other decent men would want their sons to play for. . . . Nothing escapes him on the field. He knows which players to flatter and which ones to edge with his acid tongue. He is a master of psychology who never went to college. He has infused the team with the morale necessary for winning."

McKechnie established rules for his players: in their rooms by midnight, no drinking whiskey, no poker, beer in the locker room only after wins, and no singing or laughing in the clubhouse after losses.

After one year at the helm of the Reds, McKechnie lifted Cincinnati into fourth place by winning eighty-two games, compared with fifty-six in 1937. The Reds finished six games behind the Cubs. The Reds might have fared even better had not pitcher Lee Grissom, who had been in the All-Star Game the year before, tried to steal second base and broken his leg. Grissom managed to pitch only fifty-one innings that year.

It took him only one more year to win the pennant with the team that MacPhail helped establish.

McKechnie was a by-the-book manager who played the percentages without fail. Once asked to define a book manager, he said, "A book manager? Well, what does that mean? If it means taking advantage of obvious opportunities, pulling your infield in for a play at the plate, moving it back for a double play, waiting out wild or tiring pitchers, bunting on poor-fielding pitchers, running on catchers who can't throw, sending men home on weak-armed outfielders. If that's what it means, I plead guilty. I am a book manager. Show me a manager who isn't and I'll show you a manager who loses a lot of games he ought to win."

McKechnie felt it was better to stick with the percentages consistently, rather than randomly, to get his team its best results. He believed that a bunt single was appreciated as much as a four-hundred-foot triple. He believed in "smart baseball."

But it was that style of managing that led to his downfall despite his success. In the midforties fans tired of his managerial style, seeking more excitement. Giles, the Reds' general manager, reluctantly fired McKechnie. "Those fans just forced me to fire the best manager in baseball," he said.

McKechnie also was known as an excellent handler of pitchers who helped develop them to their full potential. "He knew how to hold on to a one- or two-run lead better than any other manager," Vander Meer said.

McKechnie was a firm believer in setting a pitching rotation and sticking with it no matter which team the Reds were playing. Pitchers knew exactly which days they would be pitching. "[Pitchers] started no matter who you were playing," Vander Meer said.

Former Indians and White Sox manager Al Lopez, who was a catcher under McKechnie for Boston in 1936 and 1937, said he "learned more from McKechnie about pitching than anyone else, about trying to keep a regular rotation."

Vander Meer said all the players respected McKechnie. "And that's important because you can't play for someone you fear. McKechnie knew how to run a pitching staff. His ability to change pitchers at the right moment was uncanny. Our pitchers were always well rested."

By the end of his twenty-five-year managing career, McKechnie had taken the Reds to the World Series twice, winning in 1940. In all, he won 1,896 games and a place in the Hall of Fame. The Reds fired him in 1946, his final year of managing, after the team had compiled a 64-86 record.

If McKechnie's career was over, he certainly wasn't headed for the poorhouse. In 1935 a journeyman infielder named Randy Moore convinced McKechnie, Casey Stengel, and Al Lopez, among others, to invest in his uncle's oil-drilling business, which struck oil and made all of the investors wealthy men.

Back at Ebbets Field, Lew Riggs led off in the sixth inning by grounding to Coscarart. Then Billy Myers was called out on strikes. As Vander Meer walked to the plate for his turn at bat, he received a big ovation from the partisan fans. Vander Meer beat out a drag bunt to Coscarart that brought even greater cheers. But Frey stranded Vandy by flying out to Koy.

As Vandy warmed up to pitch the bottom of the sixth inning, he recognized that his fastball was especially quick that day. "I don't think I threw more than five curveballs over the first seven innings," he said years later. "The curve was hanging. For some reason, when I had the exceptionally good fastball I didn't have the real sharp curve."

Vander Meer first faced his counterpart, Pressnell, and coaxed him into grounding to Riggs at third, who threw him out. Next up was lead-off hitter Cuyler, who drew a walk.

Dodgers manager Grimes then sent up thirty-year-old pinch hitter Gibby Brack, who was in his second year in the Major Leagues. Brack, who was hitting .213, went down on strikes. A month later he was traded to the Philadelphia Phillies.

The next batter, Buddy Hassett, hit a slow roller that Riggs charged; he barely nipped Hassett at first in a bang-bang play—the closest play of the night to breaking up the no-hitter.

Seventh Inning

The way Johnny had been pitching before his first no-hitter gave McKechnie reassurance that he had made the right decision keeping Vander Meer when the season opened. In 1938 Vander Meer had begun to feel pretty certain he was going to get a solid shot at sticking in the Major Leagues. It happened just in time, because he was on the verge of quitting baseball. Insufficient pay and a belief that a player ought to reach the Majors within four years were burdening him. He told his teammates, "If I don't make good in '38, it's goodbye baseball for me."

On the trip to spring training in Tampa, Florida, in 1938 with Benny Borgmann, one of the Reds' Minor League managers, Vander Meer said, "I make it this time or I quit baseball. I am not going to devote the best years of my life to the minor leagues."

Borgmann asked whether Vandy thought a baseball career was worthwhile. Vandy replied, "I'd say yes, but there isn't enough money in minor league ball. The big leagues offer the chance. Young fellows should allow themselves four years in the minors and by that time should be able to realize soon enough whether or not they are fit for big league ball."

Vander Meer said he would join his brother in the milk delivery business if he left baseball. He clearly feared becoming an ex-ballplayer with an eighth-grade education who had to spend the rest of his life working in a factory as his father had.

At spring training Vander Meer worked tirelessly on his control. Despite his tendency to walk a lot of batters, he also struck out many.

"You can minimize the disadvantages of wildness if you can strike them out," Vander Meer said. "If you can pitch yourself out of trouble after you've pitched yourself in, the manager will leave you in there. I always had the ability to strike somebody out in a jam. So the wildness never bothered me mentally. Neither did three-and-two pitches. I followed Grove's philosophy in that. He always said that if you had good stuff, then on the three-and-two pitch the batter was hurting more than you were."

Because he knew he was going to throw a lot of pitches in a game, Vandy tried to keep himself in good shape. "As far as I was concerned, I was going out there to pitch eleven innings, because my nine innings were equivalent to somebody else's eleven," he said.

Vander Meer, along with two other Reds players, almost didn't make it to opening day in 1938. On March 31 Vandy, pitcher Lee Grissom, and infielder Don Lang got lost at sea when their chartered boat broke down. Their boat drifted helplessly in the Gulf of Mexico for five hours. After failing to attract the attention of passing vessels, they were finally rescued when a ship spotted an emergency flag that Vandy had rigged to a fishing pole.

In his first start that season against Pittsburgh, on April 22, 1938, he was leading 2–1 going into the third inning when his inexperience and nervousness showed. He walked two batters, got two outs, and then gave up a single and threw a ball away for an error. Before he got out of the inning, he had allowed four runs. McKechnie yanked him. Vander Meer took the loss in a 7–4 Pirates victory.

The manager put Vander Meer in the bullpen, where he pitched two games in relief. On April 27, his best outing in relief, he pitched two innings of shutout ball, giving up a hit, striking out three, and walking none.

On May 2 he wobbled to an 8–6 win over the Pirates when he returned to a starting role. He was sailing along with an 8–2 lead heading into the ninth inning when an error and three straight hits led McKechnie to send him to the showers. Reliever Joe Beggs got the last three outs to secure Vander Meer's first win of the season.

In his next start, on May 8 against the Phillies, he locked up in a pitching duel with his future teammate Bucky Walters. He matched Walters for seven shutout innings but then gave up two runs in the eighth on two walks and two singles. Vandy finished the game with six strikeouts and seven walks for a 2–0 loss. The Reds didn't come to his aid much at bat, stranding eleven runners.

McKechnie succeeded in one goal: he got a complete game out of Vander Meer. Three of the left-hander's six strikeouts came in the ninth inning. McKechnie now felt more confident that Vander Meer could finish off a game.

Despite the improvement, though, Vander Meer fell back a step when he went into the ninth inning against the Cardinals on May 14 with a 5–1 lead. The Cardinals tied it up and went on to win 7–5 in the tenth. Vandy didn't get the loss, having been taken out before the Cardinals scored their winning runs.

Then came a turning point, against the National League champion New York Giants on May 20. Vander Meer didn't know until the last minute that he was going to pitch. He'd been given only one signal: at McKechnie's request, he had pitched batting practice the day before—a sign he might pitch the next day.

McKechnie knew that Vandy liked to pitch batting practice the day before he started. "If he wants to pitch batting practice for me one day, and then goes out and stands the other team on its ear the next, there's nothing more that I can ask for." Vandy said pitching batting practice for five to seven minutes helped him loosen up for his next start.

McKechnie also allowed him to go home to spend the night with his parents, a thirty-five-mile trip from the Polo Grounds.

He even went fishing the morning of the game, suspecting that he wasn't going to pitch. He neglected to tell McKechnie that. Three months later Vander Meer commented in a *Saturday Evening Post* interview about his fishing trip, "I hope he isn't sore."

Come game time, McKechnie told Vander Meer at "the very last minute" that he was going to start. "I was calmer and more relaxed than before any game I had ever started in the majors," Vandy said. He pitched a 4–0 complete game, a five-hitter. He walked four and fanned eight. That started him on a nine-game winning streak with back-to-back no-hitters sandwiched in.

That game, he said, gave him confidence that he could pitch in the Major Leagues. "Until that game I still was a question mark," he said. "I've always believed [McKechnie's] decision to throw me in against the champion Giants at the Polo Grounds was the result of long and careful planning. But whether that was McKechnie's psychological motive I don't know. . . . I said to myself, 'You've made the grade, but don't let it go to your head. You've still plenty to learn and a far way to go.'"

On May 24 he took a small step backward. He was leading 9–1 as he took the mound in the sixth inning against the Boston Bees. Before he could get out of the inning he had allowed four runs. He was removed from the game, and his relievers couldn't hold the lead as the Bees rallied to win 10–9.

Only eighteen days later, the Bees would be hitless against Vander Meer.

The next game, the season's first night game, Vandy beat the Cardinals 2–1 in ten innings. His control was much better; he walked just two while striking out ten and giving up five base hits in the complete-game win.

General Manager Warren Giles summoned Vander Meer to his downtown Cincinnati office on May 28 to redo his contract. A contract clause stipulated that if Vander Meer was still with the team on June 15, he would receive a raise. By calling him in before that date, Giles was expressing confidence that Vander Meer would stick with the Reds.

"It's just a few days until payday, John," Giles said. "I want you to know now your old contract has been torn up. Here's your new one. Your attitude and the way you worked leave no doubt about your being on the club June 15. You are with us to stay." Vandy signed the contract, and although he did not reveal his pay, he said it was more than the total he had earned in his first three years of professional baseball.

On his next start, on June 1, he held Brooklyn to five hits in a 4–1 win. Then, on June 5, he limited the Giants to three hits as the Reds won 4–1.

The surprising thing about the game against the Giants was that he gave up two hits in the first inning—one a bunt single, the other a run-scoring double—with not another hit until Hank Leiber blooped a single in the ninth.

Vander Meer, gaining confidence, said, "I felt I could put the ball where I wanted to, and my stuff was never better." His superlative pitching performance set the stage for his next outing, the June 11 no-hitter against the Boston Bees.

Against the Dodgers, Vandy got a rest in the top of the long seventh inning—maybe too much rest, because he cooled down. Berger popped out to second baseman Johnny Hudson, who had replaced Coscarart. Ival Goodman then scorched a liner that hit Tot Pressnell on the right knee and felled him instantly. The ball rolled away for a base hit.

Brooklyn trainers worked on Pressnell for a while, eventually carrying him off on a stretcher. Pressnell wasn't seriously injured; he pitched a complete-game, 6–2 victory over the Cubs four days later.

Luke Hamlin (4-2), a lanky six-foot-two, 168-pound right-hander, replaced Pressnell, facing the Reds slugger Frank McCormick. Hamlin's nickname was "Hot Potato" because of the way he juggled the ball between pitches. Goodman promptly stole second, but Hamlin got McCormick on strikes. Lombardi was intentionally walked, and Craft hit his third straight single to score Goodman. The long inning ended when Riggs flied out to Cuyler.

After cooling his heels on the bench, Vander Meer got Phelps to hit a roller to McCormick, who beat him to first base for the out. Vandy then faced the league's top hitter, Cookie Lavagetto, in the bottom half of the seventh. Lavagetto was one percentage point ahead of the Reds catcher, at .360.

Vander Meer, losing heat off his fastball, began throwing more curves. He walked Lavagetto with one out and then walked Dolph Camilli, too. After striking out Koy, he got Durocher to hit into a forced out at second. "The curve started to work for me, and that was a break because everybody was looking for the fastball and that made me a little more effective," Vander Meer said.

Watching Vander Meer and the Reds play his new club must have been bittersweet for Larry MacPhail. After all, MacPhail had purchased Vander Meer for the Reds. Now with the Dodgers, MacPhail was with the team that had been told five years earlier that Vander Meer would never amount to a big league pitcher. He'd soon have a fit about that decision.

MacPhail was one of the brightest minds in baseball during the 1930s—and afterward, for that matter. His first Major League job had been taking over the foundering Cincinnati franchise, one of the oldest in Major League baseball, dating to 1876 when the team was known as the Red Stockings.

Baseball came relatively late in MacPhail's career. A Michigan Law School graduate, he practiced law for a while but wasn't very good at it. He tried working for a Nashville department store, where he learned marketing and merchandising skills that would serve him well in future years. After joining the army during World War I and returning home a hero, he worked in glass manufacturing, car sales, and construction, none of which brought him much profit. At the age of forty he was able to scrape together enough capital to join with several other businessmen in 1930 to buy the Double A Columbus, Ohio, Senators for $100,000. Eventually they sold the club to the Cardinals' Branch Rickey, who made MacPhail president of the newly christened Red Birds between 1930 and 1932. The Red Birds were one of the few Minor League teams to make money in those Depression years.

MacPhail made his first venture into night baseball when

twenty-one thousand fans turned out on June 17, 1931, to watch the Red Birds beat St. Paul 5–4 in eleven innings. That year the Red Birds even outdrew their parent club, the St. Louis Cardinals, by more than thirty thousand. By 1932 the Red Birds had moved into a new $400,000 stadium, which opened to a capacity crowd of seventeen thousand.

MacPhail was fired in June 1933 for lavish spending, loud public arguments with fans, incurring league fines, and flying the team on what should have been road trips. Excessive drinking might have been a problem as well.

Then along came a golden opportunity for MacPhail. A losing record and the Depression were taking a toll on the Reds and their owner, Sidney Weil. Dollars for entertainment were hard to come by in those days.

The Reds had finished last again in 1933, with a 58-94 record, while drawing the lowest attendance in the Majors at 218,281— even though Prohibition had ended and fans once again could buy a beer. The team had lost about $600,000 over a four-year period. Weil was forced to declare bankruptcy and turn the team over to a local bank.

The Reds weren't the only team that was hurting. The St. Louis Browns, the Philadelphia Phillies, and the Boston Braves were in such bad financial shape at the time that their franchises, too, were in jeopardy. Collectively, Major League teams lost $1.651 million following a 40–50 percent drop in attendance.

Still, baseball provided an escape from the depressing effects of the economy for some fans. "Like many other recreational activities," recalled Ray Robinson, a New York writer, in 2009, "people did go to the ballpark to get away from the economic horrors of empty wallets and ice boxes. I was very aware of the guys selling apples on street corners for a nickel. Along the Hudson River, you had some of these guys living in ramshackle huts in rags. So going to the ballpark was a big thing."

Fortunately for the Reds and MacPhail, he still had Rickey's backing. The bank knew nothing about running a baseball club, so at Rickey's recommendation the bank agreed to hire MacPhail to help bring the franchise back to solvency.

Not much improved in MacPhail's first year; in fact, the situation worsened. Attendance dropped to 206,773 after another last-place finish with a 52-99 record. The highest attendance reached in the previous five years had been 356,950. MacPhail recognized that he had to put a better team on the field to attract more fans. He also realized that he needed an owner with the financial wherewithal to sustain the club while he brought in better players.

First he persuaded Cincinnati entrepreneur Powel Crosley Jr. to purchase the club. Crosley was a wealthy electrical appliance maker and radio station owner who manufactured the first small American car, which bore his name. A radio that he built for his son was the forerunner of the thirty-five-dollar Crosley radio, which became the largest seller in the world; the company produced five hundred sets a day.

Crosley never expected to make any money owning the Reds, but he was swayed by MacPhail's argument that Cincinnati shouldn't lose its ball club. He paid $500,000 for the franchise, including the ballpark.

"I sure did not want to see Cincinnati become a minor league town," Crosley said. "Cincinnati is the birthplace of professional baseball, and it deserves to [be] a major league town."

When he took over ownership of the Reds, Crosley borrowed a phrase from President Franklin D. Roosevelt and promised a "New Deal" for baseball in Cincinnati. "We are in the field for better players if they can be obtained by either trade or purchase," he said. "I will rely on Mr. MacPhail's judgment as to baseball ability, and he knows that I will back him in any move he makes to put together a team which will bring credit to Cincinnati."

At MacPhail's urging, Crosley spent $450,000 on renovations and then renamed the park after himself. The park badly needed that upgrade. No improvements had been made since its opening on April 11, 1912. Redlands Field had been built for $225,000 and designed to fit into its neighborhood, a dead end at Findlay Street and Western Avenue on the site of an abandoned brickyard in the West End of Cincinnati.

Ever the supreme showman, MacPhail knew that he would have to take innovative steps to attract fans to the ballpark. Among other things, he had the park painted orange. Then he hired young women to work as ushers, dressing them in what were described as lounging pajamas. He also installed "cigarette girls" throughout the park, who were "so cute they made the customers want to smoke themselves to death," according to Reds historian Lee Allen. MacPhail was the first to offer fans a ladies' day and to play a regular-season night game.

MacPhail also wanted to broadcast the Reds games in hopes of bringing more attention to the team and drawing fans into the ballpark. Many team owners at the time worried that broadcasting games on the radio might do just the opposite and keep people away from games.

That was not as farfetched as it might sound. In those days, many fans came to the games to bet with each other; if they could hear the action on the radio, the thinking went, they could just as easily bet wherever they happened to be.

Owners decided to let the individual teams determine whether to broadcast games. The Chicago Cubs and the St. Louis Cardinals, which opted to allow game broadcasts free of charge in 1925, subsequently discovered that the broadcasts created more interest in games and thereby increased attendance. In two-team towns—Chicago, St. Louis, Boston, and Philadelphia—owners agreed not to broadcast away games, fearing that doing so might keep fans away from those cities' other teams when they played at home. New York, which had three teams—the Yankees, Dodgers, and Giants—decided to ban all broadcasts, whether at home or away.

"[The owners] finally came to the conclusion that, Depression notwithstanding, they would do nothing drastic in the way of retrenchments that would seriously affect baseball's time-honored customers or, as one owner expressed it, 'cheapen' the game," sportswriter John Drebinger wrote after the 1932 winter meetings.

One of the first actions MacPhail took in Cincinnati was to hire Red Barber, a witty, articulate Floridian who had developed a strong fan base with his down-home style of broadcasting. The twenty-six-year-old had never seen a Major League game before he joined the Reds in 1934.

Barber often carried a radio backpack that allowed him to interview fans throughout the park before the start of each game. In his first year with the Reds he broadcast thirteen home games and re-created all road games—except those in New York—in hopes of building better attendance.

As the players gave interviews and the announcers described each play, radio helped bring players' personalities to listeners in a way that newspaper articles couldn't. "MacPhail believed in [radio's] promotional power," Barber said. "He became sold on it." He said MacPhail understood how "radio [made a game] played by two teams . . . a contest involving personalities who had families, troubles, blue or brown eyes."

"And especially on days of threatening weather, when people would say, 'Well, it looks like it may rain. I'll just listen to the radio. I won't go.' They did not realize at the time the beneficial effect of radio, that it would have making families of friends." After MacPhail's broadcast in Brooklyn in 1939, Barber said, "from then on there's no question. Radio, television, more fans, more money."

Thanks to MacPhail's innovations, the Reds soon became one of nine—out of the total of sixteen—franchises making a profit. By 1936 the Reds had moved up to fifth place in the National League with a record of 74-80, increased attendance to half a million, and turned a $200,000 profit. By 1939, their pennant year, the Reds came close to having a million fans pass through their turnstiles.

In 1937 MacPhail resigned, saying, "If I stay around here much longer, I'll have a nervous breakdown." His resignation came after a number of skirmishes with police following heavy drinking bouts. Crosley wouldn't stand for it. When Crosley confronted him, MacPhail, ever the publicity hound, replied, "Boy, isn't that great publicity?"

MacPhail bounced back by landing a job with the Dodgers, where he used his formidable skills to lift the team out of its longstanding doldrums.

The game on June 15, 1938, was a major step in that direction. Vander Meer all but spoiled it. MacPhail watched the no-hit game in Ebbets Field from the press bar, along with a bartender named Hymie and the *Brooklyn Eagle* sportswriter Harold Parrott. All the other sportswriters had deserted the bar to pound out game details over their typewriters. MacPhail, who was belting down drinks and chain smoking, was wild-eyed with rage over the history-making game, his beefy red face scowling. A sportswriter once described him as "a guy who would not allow an ordinary egomaniac to get in a word edgewise."

As he watched Vandy set down one Dodger after another, a performance that brought cheers even from Dodgers fans, MacPhail grabbed a telephone and screamed into it, his raspy voice like "the call of an adult male moose," according to one sportswriter. He threatened to fire Ducky Holmes because Vander Meer had been a Dodger prospect that Holmes had released. MacPhail chose to ignore the fact that he was actually responsible for Vandy's being in Cincinnati, having signed the fireballer to his contract with the Reds.

The Reds scored their final run in the eighth when Lavagetto committed his second error of the game on a bunt by Billy Myers. Vander Meer hit a comebacker to Hamlin, who threw to Durocher to force out Myers. Frey struck out, and then Berger tripled to center, scoring Vander Meer. If the tour around the bases tired Vander Meer, it didn't show as he took the mound in the bottom half of the inning.

Manager Grimes sent up five-foot-ten, 155-pound Woody English, known for making good contact with the ball, to pinch-hit for Hamlin in the bottom of the eighth. In his career English managed three hits in eight at bats against Vander Meer.

English, thirty-two, was in the twilight of his career. In fact, the Dodgers waived him three weeks later, after he complained about not playing enough and said he was "tired of sitting on the bench."

The Reds picked up English after the Dodgers waived him. But a week later he hadn't shown up. Finally, General Manager Warren Giles received a letter from English saying that he was honeymooning in Wisconsin and he'd "rather not play until next season." The following year English went back to Brooklyn, which sold him to the Cubs, the team he broke in with.

In all, English had an eleven-year career, including one spectacular year with the Cubs. In 1930 English hit .335 and scored 154 runs. He achieved the rare feat of getting two-hundred-plus hits and more than one hundred walks. He was batting .265 with the Dodgers, with sixty-seven at bats, when he strode to the plate to face Vander Meer.

English, whose given first name was Elwood, was a well-respected, clean-cut player who neither drank nor violated curfew. He was considered by friends and foes alike to be "too nice."

Reportedly, English said to himself when he was announced as pinch hitter, "I'm not going to go up there and spoil this guy's second no-hitter." He struck out on five pitches.

The next batter, Cuyler, took a first-pitch strike and then flied out to Goodman. Johnny Hudson, who took over for Coscarart, faced Vandy for the first time. He was a .268 hitter who was two weeks shy of his twenty-sixth birthday. In his career, he managed one hit in five tries against Vandy. Hudson struck out on a 3-2 pitch.

13 Ninth Inning

In the ninth the Dodgers brought in another reliever, Vitautis Casimirus "Vito" Tamulis, (1-1) a five-foot-nine, 170-pound left-hander. Tamulis was a fun-loving wise guy known for a variety of off-speed breaking balls, including a type of "eephus" pitch, which is characterized by an unusual, high-arcing trajectory and slow velocity. He was rotund and a junkballer, meaning he had good control with no fastball throughout his career.

Tamulis set the Reds down in order, getting McCormick to fly out to Hassett, Lombardi to strike out, and Craft to fly out to Koy.

Vander Meer sat quietly in the dugout while the Reds batted. His teammates, in keeping with baseball tradition, didn't talk about the no-hitter. They also avoided Vandy. When he was pitching many of them stood on the dugout steps and cheered him on, hooting and hollering about close pitches they thought were strikes. In the dugout the players paced, their tension clearly visible.

As Vandy took the mound in the ninth, McKechnie told reliever Bucky Walters, a converted third baseman, to "sneak" down to the bullpen and warm up.

The Reds had stolen Walters from the Phillies two days earlier for catcher Spud Davis, pitcher Al Hollingsworth, and $50,000. Walters went on to a stellar nine-year career with Cincinnati in which he won 149 games and later became the Reds' manager.

While warming up, he heard booing. "I looked around, couldn't see anything going on, and continued to loosen up," he said. "And they continued to boo. The harder I threw, the louder they booed, until I realized why they were doing it. It was me they were booing, the fact that I was warming up. There was no way they wanted to see Vander Meer come out of there as long as he had that no-hitter."

Dodger fans were rooting hard for Vander Meer, especially since their team was down 6–o and history was in the making. In the inimitable style of sportswriting at that time, the *Cincinnati Time-Star's* Frank Y. Grayson wrote, "As the innings wore on and on, and Johnny was marching home with the coonskins, the multitude sensed the second classic being staged by the kid out there on the hill, and from the seventh inning on the fans were rooting with might and main for him to come through. Johnny obliged."

As he walked to the mound in the ninth inning, Vandy said he heard a noise that sounded "like a faraway buzzing of bees. I've never let the crowd's reaction bother me," he said, "but in this tense situation I must have realized in my subconscious mind what was going on."

He thought to himself, "I've got thirty good pumps left in me. I still have my good stuff, and, boy, they are going to have to hit the very best that I've got." But Vander Meer was thinking too much, and he started to press.

First up was Buddy Hassett, who had almost beat out two hits earlier in the game. On the first pitch Hassett smacked a ball back to Vander Meer, who knocked it down and then quickly found it to throw Hassett out. So far, so good. "That was probably the toughest ball to handle in either of the two ball games," Vandy said.

Next up came the dangerous Babe Phelps. Vandy tried to be too careful with the portly catcher and walked him on five pitches. Grimes wanted a faster runner in the game than Phelps and substituted Goody Rosen, a hero to Brooklyn Jews. As Peter Levine remarked in *From Ellis Island to Ebbets Field,* his study of Judaism, immigration, and American sports, "Rosen carried a double burden as both a Canadian and a Jewish ballplayer."

Levine concluded that this "doubleness ultimately prevented Rosen from achieving the stardom his talent might have warranted. Given Rosen's ethnicity and his general pugnacity, this may well be true. That said it was these same characteristics that made the cigar-smoking, Yiddish-speaking traveling garment-salesman from . . . Toronto . . . one of the most beloved Canadian baseball players of his time."

Defense, not the bat, earned Rosen a stay in the big leagues. Despite playing only as a semi-regular, Goody ended the 1938 seasons leading the National League in both fielding percentage (.989) and outfield assists (19).

Next up was Lavagetto, who was best known later in his career for breaking up a no-hitter in the 1947 World Series between the Dodgers and the Yankees. Lavagetto was at the end of his career when he was sent up as a pinch hitter to face the Yankees' Bill Bevens with two men on and two outs in the bottom of the ninth. "He was a great two-strike hitter," recalled Whitlow Wyatt, the ace of the Dodgers' pitching staff. "With men on base he was about the toughest man to get out that we had on the club."

Bevens, who had walked ten batters, was tiring. Yankees manager Bucky Harris almost yanked him. But with a no-hitter going, he didn't do it. Lavagetto hit Bevens's first pitch off the right-field wall, scoring two runs that gave the Dodgers a 3–2 win.

Neither Bevens nor Lavagetto played in a Major League game after that series.

But Cookie wasn't going to do any heroics this night against Vander Meer. Lavagetto was taking all the way. Vander Meer threw him three straight balls before rearing back and firing two strikes. But then Vandy walked him. Now there were two men on and one out. "He fired hard all through the game," Lavagetto said. "He wouldn't let up. That's why he had control problems."

Long-ball-hitting Camilli stepped in. He took a strike, then four balls, loading the bases. It was Vandy's eighth walk of the night and the third time he'd given Camilli a free pass. Coincidentally, exactly a year earlier Vandy had walked eleven batters in a 4–3 win over the Dodgers, the second-highest number of walks in a game in Vander Meer's career. As Vander Meer's control deserted him, some of his teammates looked glum, afraid to express hope, while others stood at the dugout steps and shouted encouragement.

"I started hurrying my delivery," Vander Meer said. "I wanted to get the game over fast." Camilli was the last of eight walks, a dubious honor Vandy shares with only six other pitchers (through the middle of 2010) who walked at least eight batters, including Jim Maloney, another Reds hurler, who walked ten in his 1965 no-hitter.

"What I was doing was forcing myself, trying to throw the ball harder than I could," Vander Meer recalled. But the wildness might not have hurt him as much as he thought. Cincinnati pitchers had a reputation for throwing at batters, and no one wanted to step into a wild Vander Meer fastball. It kept them loose at the plate, making it difficult to get a base hit.

Walking the bases loaded brought McKechnie to the mound. The fans booed. He wasn't going to send Vandy to the showers, was he? Vander Meer told McKechnie he was not tired, not tired at all. Few pitchers, of course, will admit they are worn out, because they want to stay in the game.

Vandy's fifteen-year-old sister Garberdina was wringing her hands in the stands. "That was scary. That really brought everybody real quiet, and I thought maybe he would lose it then."

His mother, sitting behind the third base dugout, was a nervous wreck. "I couldn't watch the last two innings. I turned my head away and prayed all the Dodgers would strike out," she said. The crowd rose up as one, yelling, "Don't take him out. Don't take him out." Second baseman Lonnie Frey, a three-time All-Star, wondered, "when in the world is he going to get the ball over the plate."

McKechnie tried to calm Vander Meer. "You're trying to put too much on the ball, John. Just get it over there. Those hitters up there are scared to death." It was unlikely McKechnie would take him out of the game with a 6–0 lead.

Lombardi told him to pretend they were playing catch. "I'll hold up my mitt," he said, "and you hit it. Forget there's anyone else in this ballpark but you and me." Lombardi also told him, "You're either going to give up a hit or you're not, so blaze that fast one in there." Vander Meer nodded and went back to work.

Although McKechnie didn't say much, "it was enough," Vander Meer said. "It wasn't what he said so much, but the way he said it that brought back my waning confidence and control." He decided to use his best pitch, his fastball. "In life you either do it or you don't when you have enough spots. I wasn't going to regret something later in life, like throwing a change of pace. I was going to power river. That was my best pitch and that's what I was going to throw. And I did."

Next up was Ernie Koy, who two weeks earlier had three of the Dodgers' four hits in a Vander Meer shutout. He was a .299 hitter for the season. After Vandy threw a strike, Koy hit the next pitch on the ground to Reds third baseman Lew Riggs. Riggs knew he couldn't double up the speedy Koy, so he carefully threw the ball home to Lombardi to force out Rosen and preserve the shutout. "It was fast thinking by Riggs," Vander Meer said, "going for the sure thing rather than the long double play because Koy could run."

Lombardi wisely decided against trying to throw to first in an attempt to get Koy. He saw Koy running inside the baseline. He knew Koy was fast, and because Koy was running inside the line, a throw from home to first might hit him. So he held the ball rather than taking a chance on either hitting Koy or throwing the ball into right field.

At this point MacPhail was only halfway watching the game as he yelled into the phone. He should have been happy. Everything was going right for the majordomo. He had pulled in more than $100,000 in gate receipts for the game, a sum that would help turn around the financial fortunes of the Dodgers. When the year was done, the Dodgers had made money for the first time since 1920. His night also was an artistic success, except for that damned Vander Meer.

All MacPhail could think about was Ducky Holmes, that idiot in the Dodger farm system who had released Vander Meer because he was too wild with his pitches. "Four years ago that dumb son-of-a-bitch released Vander Meer outright when he was managing one of our farm teams," MacPhail yelled at no one in particular. "Without permission, too. Except for that fathead, Vandy would still be a Dodger, and the whole show would have been ours tonight."

MacPhail never reached Holmes. Probably just as well, for as MacPhail stormed out of the pressroom, he was handed a telegram. He read the telegram, crumpled it into a ball, and threw it toward the bartender. Hymie, the bartender, picked it up and read it. It said, "Congratulations on your big night game success. Hope you win. Ducky Holmes."

Holmes's fate has been lost to the ages, except for his suspension later that year for 120 games because he punched an umpire in the nose—the third or fourth time he had gotten into a physical fight with an umpire.

Vandy now had only one more batter to face to complete the second no-hitter—the scrappy Leo Durocher, who, although he was hitting only .256, was tough in the clutch. "Durocher was a loud guy; he had a big mouth," Frey remembered. "We didn't want him to get a hit, of all the players on the team, that's for sure."

In a playing and managing career that spanned nearly five decades, from 1925 to 1973, Leo Durocher was one of the game's fiercest competitors and hardest losers. Combative, explosive, outspoken, fanatical, insolent, ruthless—these are just a few of the adjectives used to describe the man whose credo was "nice guys finish last."

Durocher was the scourge of National League umpires for his relentless heckling and obscenity-laden tirades. Umpire Bill Stewart, who was behind the plate the night of Vander Meer's second no-hitter, once said about Durocher, "From the bench, his rasping voice out of the side of his mouth and his gestures made you want to cleave him with a meat ax." The bantam rooster was no one to mess with. Sportswriter Harold Parrott said, "When you cross Durocher you had better be sure that your own jockstrap and cup are in place."

Waite Hoyt, a future Hall of Fame pitcher, once noted that Durocher was a .400 hitter—.200 batting right-handed and .200 batting left. Babe Ruth called him the "All-American out." Durocher detested Ruth for that statement and ignored him in the Dodgers' dugout prior to the game.

In recounting the game five days later, the *New York Times*'s esteemed sports columnist John Kieran wrote, "Durocher was the man. Just imagine a hitter like Durocher ruining a performance like that (which was exactly what everybody in the park was imagining)."

Vander Meer grabbed the rosin bag, threw it down, looked into the lights, and then tugged at his hat, pulling it low on his forehead as if to give himself a tougher look. Bent at the waist, with his glove hand dangling and his left arm behind him, he peered in at Lombardi's signal. Then he reared back, kicked his leg high, and fired the ball. "Ball," called out umpire Stewart. Lombardi called time and lumbered out to the mound. "Now," he told Vander Meer, "you're either going to give up a hit or you're not. So buzz that fast one right through there." Vandy then threw a strike.

With the count one and one, Durocher smacked a pitch deep to right field that brought the crowd to its feet. But the ball hooked foul. You could almost hear the collective sigh of relief. One ball, two strikes. On the next pitch Vander Meer thought he nipped the outside corner of the plate, a pitch that would have ended the game. Lombardi jumped up from his crouch, thinking that Vander Meer had done the impossible. But Stewart called it a ball. The crowd let out a gasp, not wanting to believe the call.

Lombardi let Stewart know what he thought of the call. His teammates on the Cincinnati bench hooted and hollered at Stewart. Vander Meer, however, remained quiet, trying to compose himself. "There was no sense in upsetting myself, not in that spot," Vander Meer said. Years later, Vander Meer recalled that Lombardi threw the ball back to him so hard it "almost broke my hand."

A short man, Stewart may have had trouble seeing the pitch because of Lombardi's hulking presence. "When you screen an umpire, it's an automatic ball," Vander Meer said. He thought that maybe Lombardi came out of his crouch too quickly and Stewart had to call a ball. Two balls, two strikes.

Said Stewart, a veteran of four years behind the plate: "I was pulling for the kid as much as anybody. I could feel the pressure of the crowd and the players on me. I was mighty lonely out there. Everybody wanted it to be a third strike."

Durocher was still alive. On the next pitch he hit an easy fly ball to center fielder Harry Craft, a superb fly catcher.

Lonny Frey looked up into the lights and let out a sigh of relief as he saw Craft, playing shallow center field, running in to easily grab Durocher's fly ball. "Boy, did [he] squeeze that ball," Frey said.

"If it had to be hit to the outfield, he's the guy I wanted to catch it," Vandy said.

Back in Cincinnati, fans listening to the half-hour reports of the game on the radio heard the announcer say, "We may have a little surprise for you. The game is over, but that is not all. Vandy has hung up a new record—another no-hit game." Cheers rose from living rooms and saloons throughout Cincinnati at the news.

In Richmond, Indiana, a cigar-store proprietor shook his head in bewilderment after he learned that the odds he had given two young customers of 100–1 that Vandy would pitch another no-hitter would cost him a hundred dollars.

Durocher recalled twenty-three years later that he would never forget that time at bat. "I wanted a hit so bad I could taste it. I had nothing against Vandy, but I still wanted the hit."

In his 1975 autobiography, *Nice Guys Finish Last*, Durocher, he of the overblown ego, gave this account: "There I was facing Vander Meer with two out. And I hit a ball just as good as I could hit it, a line drive, which Harry Craft, their fine center fielder, caught right off his shoe tops."

On the fiftieth anniversary of the game, Durocher told the *Los Angeles Times* that he hit a "mediocre" fly ball to center field. "It was what you would call a semi-line drive," he said. "It wasn't that I hit the ball hard or anything. Let me say it was between hitting it good and hitting it bad. Craft caught it about two feet off the ground."

Craft disputed that. "The truth was, it was like a feather on a feather bed," he said.

Tommy Holmes of the *Brooklyn Eagle* wrote, "Out and upward sailed the ball. It seemed to hang suspended against the blue-black sky, white and small as Harry Craft dashed in from the deep reaches of the outfield. Craft stopped and raised his hands and the ball dropped slowly—it seemed—into the center fielder's glove."

After Durocher flied out, Stewart ran out to Vander Meer, telling him, "John, I blew that pitch. If you hadn't got him out I was the guy to blame for it." Vander Meer later replied, "I've often wondered if Leo had gotten a base hit if he [Stewart] would have run out there and said that then."

Stewart noted that Vander Meer was getting his curve over for strikes. "Earlier in the season I worked a game Vander Meer pitched, and his curve was continually breaking into the dirt," he said. "But this time it was cutting that inside corner, as was his fastball. Mind you, Vander Meer was getting by without a change of pace, but he was mixing his hopping fastball with a better curve than he ever showed me before and using good judgment, too. That's what gave him the no-hitter—good judgment on pitches, and for that Lombardi rates a hand. In a game like that the catcher is almost as instrumental as the pitcher." Years later, Vandy said about Lombardi, "He caught every pitch in those two no-hitters, and I never shook him off once."

Lombardi recalled how difficult it was to catch Vander Meer when he was wild. "You never knew where the ball was going to end up when he was pitching," he said. "When you caught Vandy for nine innings you knew you were in a game. All you'd want to do after that was go home to bed."

Lombardi called fastball after fastball through the seventh inning, but then the catcher thought Vander Meer had begun to tire. So Lombardi changed to curve balls even though they were harder to catch. "I felt I had more of a chance to catch the fastball than the curve. . . . he could bounce the curve," Lombardi said.

Vander Meer may have walked eight, but Dodger batters hit only five balls out of the infield. "You know, you're concentrating so much on the game that, when it's finished, you don't know what you're doing for some time," Vander Meer said.

Durocher had nothing but praise for Vandy's effort. "Vander Meer had more speed and stuff tonight than I've ever seen in baseball," Durocher said.

Fifty years later, he said,

He was fast, all right, but many others have been a lot faster than he was. Today a lot of pitchers bring it around 90–95 mph. Vandy was about 90, sometimes 92. Once in a while, he might turn a couple loose at 94. Besides his fastball, he had a good curve and a good motion, with a high kick. The way he kicked his leg up, his delivery was so deceptive that you really had to concentrate to keep your eye on the ball. On top of that, he was so wild that you had to stay loose. You couldn't afford to dig in on him.

If a pitcher has to be extremely sharp to pitch a no-hitter, he also needs some breaks and good fielding from his teammates. "I don't care what professional sport you're playing," Vander Meer said years later. "You got to get breaks. But the true answer to getting breaks is you got to take advantage of them. If you don't . . . there's no advantage of getting breaks. So we always say in pro sports, you have to create your own breaks."

The Dodgers' Babe Phelps thought Vander Meer had some luck. "We hit a few balls that if they were hit six inches either way would have been base hits," he said on the fiftieth anniversary of Vander Meer's feat. "But give the guy credit. He took advantage of the situation."

As the crowd erupted when Durocher flied out, Vander Meer's teammates hugged and slapped him and then tried to help him get off the field, away from the clutches of the exuberant crowd. McKechnie, too, sought to protect his star pitcher. "Save him," he shouted, and two of Vandy's biggest teammates, six-foot-three, 205-pound Paul Derringer and six-foot-six, 230-pound Jim Weaver, escorted him off the field.

As sportswriter Lou Smith of the *Cincinnati Enquirer* described it, "Bedlam broke loose. It looked like a college flag rush as the frenzied fans streamed through the exits and vaulted over the railings to pay tribute to baseball's newest No. 1 hero. They encircled the dog-tired youngster before he could cross the left-field foul line. And for a minute it looked as though he was going to pass out. He appeared to be in a haze. But he quickly recovered, and with the aid of his teammates and several dozen of New York's finest, managed to make the dugout."

Smith continued, "Even [in the dugout] he was not safe from autograph hunters, who pushed his teammates and the cops away like they were so many corn husks. But the young Dutchman had recovered his equilibrium and beat a hasty retreat to the dressing room, where he received the congratulations of his teammates behind closed doors."

Sportswriter Henry C. Schwartz of the *Paterson (NJ) Evening*

News was blocked from entering the locker room but managed to ask Frank McCormick how Vander Meer felt. "He couldn't say anything," McCormick replied. "We did all the popping off." The fans clustered around Vander Meer's family as well for at least fifteen minutes after the game. As the fans mobbed Vander Meer's father, one cut off his tie. Police had to escort the pitcher's parents to their car. "The funny thing was," Vandy said, "Dad didn't know very much about baseball and was probably the only person in the ballpark who didn't know I'd set a record. He was wondering what all the fuss was about." His proud mother managed to tell sportswriter Hy Turkin that she "was never so happy in my life. Just think, it seems only yesterday I bought my little Johnny his first baseball suit. He was only four years old then."

Not only was the game one of a kind, but by today's standards it was remarkable that it took so little time—two hours and twenty-two minutes. Moreover, Vandy's first no-hitter took one hour and forty-five minutes. In the Major Leagues today, most games finish in a little under three hours. In 2002 postseason games averaged three hours and twenty-five minutes. The Red Sox and the Yankees seem to take even longer. For example, the first three Red Sox–Yankees games at the start of the 2010 season took 3:46, 3:48, and 3:21. In Vander Meer's time hitters rarely left the batter's box, and pitchers went into their windup almost immediately after getting the ball back and signals from the catcher.

In addition, few pitchers complete games today. The Major League leader in complete games in 2009 was Toronto's Roy Halladay with nine. In 1938 Bobo Newsom started forty games and completed thirty-one. Vander Meer started twenty-nine games and finished sixteen.

Games are further delayed when managers change pitchers as often as they do today, often lifting a pitcher after he's thrown about a hundred pitches. Although pitch counts weren't kept with any regularity in the 1930s, pitchers often threw 125 or more. Vandy surely pitched more than that when he pitched fifteen innings of a nineteen-inning game in 1946.

No record exists today on how many pitches Vandy threw the night of his second no-hitter. But he issued eight walks—a minimum of thirty-two pitches to those batters for sure; threw seven strikeouts—a minimum of twenty-one pitches; and threw twenty other put-outs—a minimum of twenty pitches. That's a total seventy-three pitches minimum. That figure does not include strikes to batters who walked or balls to batters who struck out. It also does not include balls and strikes to batters who took pitches before hitting the ball into outs, nor does it include foul balls hit after two strikes.

Vander Meer threw 13 pitches in the eighth inning and 27 in the ninth inning alone, the only innings in which pitches were counted in that game. That's 40 pitches in two innings. It is likely that Vandy threw at least 125 pitches. And the game still only took two hours and twenty-two minutes.

After the Game 14

In the locker room an exhausted Vander Meer said he had better "stuff" when he beat the Giants on June 5. "They got a lucky hit off me in the ninth," he said. "I was afraid the Dodgers would get lucky, too. Now I realize I was lucky. With all that wood swinging up there you never know when a fellow is going to slice a peanut hit off you or scalp the top of the ball for a horseshoe dribbler." (Vander Meer probably said "horseshit," but the reporter couldn't use that word in the newspaper.)

McKechnie called it his biggest thrill in thirty-one years in baseball. "I cannot tell you how Johnny happened to be so good in those two games. It's beyond me, and probably no one will know the answer. But I can say he's a fine pitcher and has the stuff."

McKechnie said Lombardi got too little credit when praise was handed out to Vander Meer. "Sure he was great," McKechnie said of Vander Meer. "But it seems like everybody forgets that Ernie Lombardi had to catch two perfect games if Vander Meer was to pitch them."

MacPhail didn't blame the Dodgers' poor performance on the lights. "It's fortunate that Vander Meer proved he can pitch no-hitters in the daytime, or everybody would be blaming it on the lights," he said. That certainly was the right statement to make if the Dodgers wanted to keep playing at night. Outfielder Ernie Koy agreed. "I didn't have any trouble with [the lights], but I couldn't get the base hits," Koy said.

One Dodger even grumbled, "This screwy schedule gets your stomach shot to hell. You're eating a steak dinner at midnight and colliding with yourself getting up for batting drill the next day."

Years later, Lavagetto said, "It was tough hitting against him. It's always tough hitting against a fastballer under the lights. And the lights were new to us then. But Vander Meer was good enough that game to pitch a no-hitter under any conditions."

Not giving the lights some credit for Vandy's success would be like saying his teammates didn't help, either. Of course the lights helped. While Vander Meer was sharp that night, the Dodgers hadn't played a single game under the lights, while the Reds had. When luck plays a big part in a no-hitter, every little edge a pitcher gets—and the lights were an edge—would help him achieve the no-hitter. Was it coincidence or magic that the first back-to-back no-hitters came at a night game? Maybe both.

In the clubhouse Vandy flopped wearily down on a bench. McKechnie sat quietly by while Vander Meer's teammates hugged him and patted him on the back. Derringer told Vander Meer, "You sure are making it tough for the rest of us pitchers." Wally Berger threw his hat in the air and exclaimed, "Whew! At last I'm with a real ball club."

While trainer Doc Rohde rubbed his arm in the clubhouse, Vander Meer said, "I was much faster tonight than last Saturday. My curve ball was breaking sharper." Johnny also revealed that he knew he was pitching a no-hitter. "And I wanted to get it. . . . No one needed to tell me I was on my way to a no-hitter tonight. I knew it all the time. And I was trying so hard to make certain of it. Pressed too much and my control slipped at times." After the fifth inning, he said, "I just kept fogging 'em in," although he admitted he was a little tired in the last two innings, "and it certainly was a relief to me when I turned around and saw Harry [Craft] circling under Durocher's fly."

What he apparently didn't know until he reached the locker room was that he had accomplished a unique feat. "If I'd known it had never been done before, it would have put more heat on me."

Harry Hartman, WCPO's veteran sportscaster, was the only nonplayer or coach in the clubhouse after the game. He had been sitting on the Reds' bench during the crucial ninth inning. "The tension was terrific," he said. After the final out Hartman was almost trampled as Vandy's teammates rushed to protect him. Hartman accompanied them into the clubhouse, where the players broke into wild joy. "Vandy was almost crushed with other players hugging him," Hartman said. "He in turn expressed his gratitude to Lombardi by kissing the big Italian on the ear."

A while later Dodger players, led by former Reds player Kiki Cuyler, came into the clubhouse to congratulate Vander Meer.

MacPhail had calmed down from his tirade by the time a *Cincinnati Enquirer* sportswriter reached him. "Fact of the matter is, I've got mixed emotions about this," MacPhail said. "In one way I'm proud of the kid. Why I was even pulling for him to come through—after there were two outs in the ninth inning. On the other hand, I wanted to see our club win, of course." MacPhail recounted how he had paid $12,000—actually $17,500—for Vandy while he was in the Minor Leagues. "I'm not saying what I'd pay for him now," MacPhail said.

Then, in a bit of prophecy, MacPhail noted, "Everybody, of course, is going to be asking whether he will last or blow up like a lot of other young pitchers who started out well. I don't know why he shouldn't last. But, then there [have] been a lot of fastball pitchers like him who have thrown their arms off in a pretty short time."

Vander Meer reflected years later that the no-hitters came too fast in his young career. "I was more confused than thrilled. All the publicity, the attention, the interviews, the photographs, were too much for me," he said. "They swept me off my feet too far to let me have time to think about the games themselves." He called it the haziest period of his life—"sort of like a dream."

Vander Meer was besieged by offers to endorse products ranging from breakfast food to clothespins. He was offered motion picture and advertising contracts right and left. "Chiselers also are trying to horn in," the *Cincinnati Enquirer* reported.

Reds general manager Warren Giles asked Johnny's father what he thought about the game. "Baseball is all right," he replied, "but we wish Johnny wouldn't pitch on Sunday. Johnny's always been a good boy and I hope success won't spoil him. This is the first big league game I ever saw, but not the first no-hit game I've seen my boy pitch."

Vander Meer took his time showering and dressing after the game with the hope that the crowd would disperse. He told reporters he was going fishing the next day, "and I'm not telling you where. I got a permit today from the mayor of Newark to fish in a special spot where the trout are supposed to be biting."

Postgame 15

Vandy arrived at his parents' house at 1:00 a.m., but he didn't get any sleep. He stayed up all night, sipping a ginger ale and talking with friends about the game until it was time to go fishing at 5:00 a.m. He had set a date two months earlier to go fishing with Joe Rutter, a New Jersey state trooper. Rutter didn't expect Vander Meer to show up, yet the pitcher walked into a diner for breakfast right on time.

The morning after the game hordes of fans, agents with endorsement offers, sportswriters, and photographers mobbed the New York hotel where the Reds where staying. After discovering that Vander Meer had stayed at his parents' home they took off for Midland Park.

When the crowd arrived at the Vander Meer home they were greeted with barks from a liver-and-white-colored pointer. His father came to the door to greet the reporters. "My, but this is a queer turn for my family," he said.

In his thick Dutch accent, Jacob Vander Meer told them, "You see reporters and men from the papers. They have been around my house now since three-thirty this morning. So John he cannot sleep a bit. At five o'clock this morning he take his fishing rod, slip out of the back door and go fishing on a lake where nobody can find him." He said Johnny had to hike in to the lake. "My John is a good hiker," Jacob said. "He loves to hike fast. Big lungs, my boy he has."

His son was fishing on a private lake about eight miles away. "And he will not return until after dark, and I hope by then these men have gone, so that we will have some peace and quiet . . . like John likes, like my family and I like."

Reporters asked him whether he was happy with his son's baseball life. "Yes," he answered, "the baseball is fine. I mean better in his own life. He is a fine boy. Smokes only a little and never drinks nothing—maybe a glass of beer once in a long while. But John never drinks hard liquor. It would kill his mother, hurt me if he would do that. A fine boy like my boy has no time for drinking. He is happy running the deer in the woods. John like much of green vegetables and broiled chicken [his favorite meal], eat good, sleep good, live good and peaceful."

His mother told reporters she was the happiest woman in Midland Park "and maybe the world, but all I want to do is get away from you fellows. You make me nervous." And then Jacob Vander Meer ended the interview. "I like to see Johnny get ahead," he said, "but I don't want to give you any story. Johnny does his own talking. And besides, it's almost twelve o'clock, and I haven't fed the chickens."

Newsmen hung around the two-story frame house hoping Johnny would drop by. Finally the family left for the day to avoid the hubbub. By the time Vandy and Rutter finished fishing and returned home, the reporters and photographers had left. Vander Meer's sister, Garberdina, remembered, "I think my dad had two bushels of flashbulbs to pick up in the yard."

That afternoon Gabe Paul, McKechnie, and Giles drove to New Jersey to pay a visit to Vander Meer's parents. "I'll never forget when we got to the place," Paul said. "I saw a sign, 'Fresh Eggs for Sale.'" Were the Vander Meers farmers? "No, we weren't farmers," Vander Meer said. "My father had a couple of hundred chickens, that's all."

Vandy was not particularly fond of those chickens. "Every Saturday morning my dad made me go out behind our house and clean up the chicken coops. What an awful job that was."

That night, after Vander Meer returned from his fishing trip, his mother and father entertained their future daughter-in-law, Lois Stewart, and two reporters for the *Cincinnati Post*, one of them also a stringer for the *Sporting News*. Jacob sat on a piano bench in the living room and pointed to a framed certificate on the wall commemorating his son being named Minor League player of the year by the *Sporting News*. "There's room on the other side of that same wall for a certificate saying Johnny is the No. 1 player of the big leagues. I hope he can win that sometime, so the two will balance each other." Six months later Jacob received his wish, when the *Sporting News* named his son the Major League player of the year in 1938. He proudly hung that certificate as well, positioning it so it could be seen by anyone who walked through the front door.

Vandy received numerous offers for radio appearances and endorsements. Even the town of Midland Park contemplated changing its name to Vander Meer. The mayor of Durham, where he had played Minor League ball, urged him to run for mayor of that town. President Roosevelt sent him a congratulatory telegram. Back in Cincinnati sportswriters were giving him nicknames like "The Dutch Master" and "Vander Meeracle." One sportswriter went so far as to propose erecting a statue of Vander Meer in Garfield Square to replace the one of the former president. The Ohio legislature halted debate on a relief program to honor "the newly crowned king of pitching."

Reds assistant general manager Frank Lane said ticket orders were piling up after the no-hitters. "Nothing like it in the history of the club," he said. Lane said he was roused out of bed at 1:30 a.m. by a telephone call from a fan in Durham, who "fairly yelled that 'We'll bring half the town up if you'll just give us a little more than forty-eight hours'" notice when Vander Meer would pitch next. Lane said that ticket sales for the next night game had already sold a thousand to fifteen hundred extra tickets.

Manager Bill McKechnie also stood to gain from Vandy's accomplishment. If the Reds drew 450,000 for the season, he would receive a bonus of $5,000. If they finished in the first division, he would get another $5,000. "And a few more games like Vander Meer has been pitching recently, well—we may be there," Lane said.

Vandy was besieged with requests for autographs, which he rarely refused. "It's a good thing he writes with his right hand, or he would never have been able to pitch," a friend noted.

While his accomplishment stood alone—and still stands alone—he joined the select company of being one of four pitchers at that time to hurl two no-hitters in his career. The others were Theodore Breitenstein, Cy Young, and Christy Mathewson.

Did Vandy think he could pitch three in a row? "I can't say I'll be out there for another no-hitter next time," he told sportswriters. "I'll just start out like I did last night and pitch my natural game. Then we'll have to see what happens." He told another sportswriter, "I like to pitch no-hitters. I pitched five of them on the Paterson sandlots. If I live long enough I'd like to pitch five in the Big Top."

Reds baseball announcer Red Barber remembered Vander Meer's big night well. He had to change the listing of his telephone number to his wife's name because of it.

Barber's telephone number was listed under Walter Red Barber because he thought he should stay in touch with his listeners. The night Vander Meer pitched his second no-hitter, the telephone rang off the hook. When news of the sensational pitching effort came over the Associated Press wire and radio programs broadcast it to listeners, they wanted to talk about it with someone, anyone. Many of them chose Red Barber.

Despite reports to the contrary, Barber did not announce the game from Brooklyn. Radio broadcasts had been banned by New York teams for fear that it would hurt attendance. Neither was Western Union allowed to send reports of the games for re-creations in places like Cincinnati.

"I don't remember exactly what time that night the word came through," Barber said, "but I would guess it was between ten and eleven. It set that staid old town on its ear. Cincinnati went berserk."

Along the "Rhine"—the canal near the Ohio River—celebrators in beer gardens leaped for joy over the news. As they consumed more beer they talked more and more about Vander Meer's feat. "After a while it seemed that nothing would do but that everybody in Cincinnati had to phone old Red Barber and talk to him about Vander Meer's second no-hitter," Barber said. He hadn't seen the no-hitter and knew no more than the revelers did. "But they called and they called and they called and that phone kept ringing until four in the morning. One caller after the other, strangers in beer halls, drunks, over and over again. It was a very long night."

Barber said that years later he still came across people who told him they had listened to the game on the radio. As with many major sporting events, the people who claimed to have seen Vandy's sterling night totaled in the hundreds of thousands. Yet it all happened in the relative obscurity of cozy Ebbets Field.

Forty-one years later Barber attended the annual meeting of the Florida Association of Broadcasters and, off the cuff, recreated the last half of the ninth inning of the second no-hitter. "Now," Barber said, "on the brink of greatness, unprecedented greatness, he's gone wild [walking the bases loaded.]" And he proceeded to once again bring to life that climactic moment when Vander Meer—"Van-da-me-ah," as he pronounced it in his Alabama accent—pitched to Durocher, and Durocher flied out.

Two days after his second no-hitter, the *Cincinnati Enquirer* editorialized, "It's only fair to warn Adolf Hitler that if he does march into Czechoslovakia one of these fine hot days, he won't have the headlines in these parts if the Reds are playing—and particularly if Johnny Vander Meer is in the box."

Not to be outdone, Bailey Millard penned a poem for the June 20 *Los Angeles Times* titled "No Hits, No Runs." In part it read,

He is history's and fame's
Only hurler to win ever
    Two successive no-hit games.
O valiant deeds in battle
    Let poets chant and cheer,
But I glory in the triumph
    Of Johnny Vander Meer

When the Reds returned from their road trip on July 1, a crowd of an estimated five thousand fans welcomed them home despite a steady rain. The fans cheered every player as he stepped from the train to a flag-bedecked platform. They saved their biggest cheers for Vander Meer.

Before his next start, Reds officials asked Vander Meer if he would be willing to change his jersey number from 33 to 00, but he refused.

FBI director J. Edgar Hoover wrote Vander Meer a letter, mailed three days after the no-hitter, that was simply addressed, Mr. Johnny Vander Meer, Midland Park, New Jersey. The postman had no trouble delivering it. Ever the publicity-seeking G-man, Hoover said he took time out from heading the investigation into the kidnapping of a five-year-old Princeton, Florida, boy to take a peek at the newspapers in Miami, where he learned of Vandy's no-hitters. Hoover called the no-hitters thrilling and extended his congratulations "on this remarkable feat."

Vandy also was named honorary mayor of Tampa, Florida, where the Reds held spring training. Bellhops at the McAlpin Hotel agreed not to accept tips from Vander Meer while he was staying there, to show their appreciation for his no-hitters.

He also rejected having a new park in his hometown named after him. "I don't want to be pointed out as the guy who keeps the tax rate up thirty or forty points for the upkeep of a park named after me," he said. "And perhaps that might happen after I've hung up my glove in a few years." Vandy thought the $8,000 to $10,000 price tag for the park was too expensive. "Anyway, it's too big an honor for me and too big an undertaking."

Vandy was overwhelmed by the sensation his back-to-back no-hitters had created. "Yes, I've learned a lot about heroes," he said. "A fellow sure has to keep his head. After I pitched those two no-hitters I did fairly well for a spell, but in the last few games I haven't had much more than a reputation. Maybe you'll think this is a lot of Dutch dupe, but I'd like to swap those no-hitters for a couple of well-pitched winning games right now. I'm too wild and throw too many fastballs. And it seems I get into all my pitching trouble after two are out."

In the four games just before the no-hitters, Vander Meer was virtually untouchable. He pitched four complete games, one a ten-inning affair, allowed a total of three runs on eighteen hits, struck out thirty, and walked ten. After the no-hitters, his record was 7-2.

Vander Meer became popular with business endeavors that wanted to capitalize on his fame to endorse their products. He received so many offers of all kinds that he used Warren Giles as his business manager. Giles would accept only one dollar in compensation. "I can't estimate how much has been offered to Johnny," Giles said.

Giles asked Vander Meer, "What do you want to be, a pitcher like Walter Johnson, Carl Hubbell, Christy Mathewson or some of the other greats, or do you want to attract attention as a freak or a sideshow type of player?"

Vander Meer replied, "Baseball is my business, and that comes first with me. I have no desire to do anything that will interfere in the slightest with my baseball career."

Vandy trusted Giles implicitly. "If Mr. Giles said something to you—there's not very many general managers in the big leagues whose word I would trust, and I found out that later," Vander Meer said. "But if Mr. Giles ever made a commitment to me personally . . . I'd take Mr. Giles' word anytime. If he gave me his word, that's all I had to have. . . . I think Mr. Giles was probably the fairest business man that I was ever associated with."

Giles made sure he signed no contracts "that might possibly

make me appear cheap, a nickel grabber," Vander Meer said. Reds owner Powel Crosley Jr. often put up money that Giles turned down on unscrupulous offers so that Vander Meer didn't lose income. "Johnny is taking his time," Giles said. "He says that he is primarily a baseball player and does not want a lot of tinsel and ballyhoo."

Giles estimated that Vandy earned $10,000 for his endorsements. "We could make $50,000 if we didn't insist on only the most dignified offers," Giles said. Giles said Vander Meer received more than one hundred offers and accepted fifteen. The Reds bought him a paid-up annuity worth $5,000, "and that actually was the most important thing he got out of it," Giles said.

"In terms of money, advertisers didn't have much to throw around [because of the Depression]," Vander Meer said years later. "It's the old story: Everybody was born twenty-five years too soon. But I have no complaints; I did all right for the time."

He also turned down several lucrative offers for nightclub appearances. "Yeah, I've suddenly become a businessman," he said. "It's all wrong though. My business is pitching and no one is going to lead me astray. I can use the money all right. I have to live, same as anyone else. But I'm not going to become a freak."

Giles went so far as to seek money from sportswriters to interview Vandy. All writers, except those for Cincinnati papers, had to agree to pay 50 percent of their earnings from their stories. Cincinnati sportswriters could interview Vandy without charge. Giles also said that even orphanages seeking autographed balls for the purpose of raffling them must pay for the balls.

Giles said he didn't want out-of-town sportswriters to make money at Vander Meer's expense. "I'm looking after these affairs so that everyone won't be riding on Mr. Vander Meer's wagon for profit. These writers are not active for Mr. Vander Meer's sake," Giles said. "They're writing the articles for their own profit. Mr. Vander Meer achieved the fame that made it possible. It's only right that he should share."

A sportswriter asked if the stories hadn't helped keep Vandy's fame alive. Giles responded, "You bet they do, but they're not doing it for Johnny. . . . If that program is wrong, it is my fault and not Mr. Vander Meer's fault. I'm just trying to look after his welfare."

Nationally known sports columnist Westbrook Pegler chimed in that several sportswriters were "deeply hurt, feeling that Vander Meer has snapped at a hand extended to pet him and munched it clear up to the shoulder. Not overpaid, at best, some of them have had a chance to make a few dollars spreading the fame of a hero, and the young man's demands would cut their ten-dollar and twenty-dollar fees in half."

Giles responded that while the fees would cut into the money the out-of-town sportswriters would receive, had Vander Meer not pitched himself to fame the article would not be written at all. Giles said he wouldn't charge Cincinnati sportswriters because their newspapers were trying to increase circulation.

Giles wanted to make sure Vandy received money for stories like one printed in the *Saturday Evening Post* on August 27, 1938, titled, "Two Games Don't Make a Pitcher." Pictures showed him going through his pitching motion. Similar stories ran in *Life* and *Look*. Many youngsters no doubt kept those magazines in their rooms, mimicking Vandy's windup in front of bedroom mirrors. One of them was Bert Shepard, a high school boy in 1938. Shepard's professional baseball career was cut short by World War II, during which he lost a leg. Yet he still managed to return to baseball, playing in one game for the Washington Senators in 1947.

Pitcher Junior Thompson, who joined the Reds for the 1939 season, recalled that some of Vander Meer's teammates were rankled by the arrangement with Giles and the attention their teammate received in his rookie year, although they all liked him. Third baseman Lew Riggs called him "a fine kid. We all feel the same about it. He hasn't a big head—and this thing hasn't changed him."

Fans suddenly became crazy about the Reds. Farmers, who often found out about games in the next day's newspaper, installed radios in their tractors so they could follow the team. A woman from Durham asked the Reds office to give her forty-eight hours' notice whenever Vandy was to pitch.

Baseball historian Curt Smith wrote, "Play-Doh, Formica, and floating soap were invented in Cincinnati. Dr. Albert Sabin ripened his oral polio vaccine, and Dr. Henry Heimlich began his life-saving maneuver. At the moment, a Rhinelander—Germans comprised a quarter of the city's population—would have traded them all for a Vandy handshake and a ball."

A sportswriter asked McKechnie when he saw the potential in Vander Meer. "I liked Johnny from the first look I got at him in the spring training camp," he said. "I told our reporters then that we had the 1938 pitching sensation of the major leagues in Vander Meer. Why, he was knocking the bats right out of the Detroit Tigers' hands in exhibition games."

The writer asked McKechnie whether he thought all the attention would hurt Vandy's efforts on the mound. "Not at all," he said. "Johnny doesn't show it, and he's still not over the excitement, but don't you think for one minute that it will affect him in any way." Maybe yes, maybe no. Vander Meer had an 8-8 record the rest of the year and finished 15-10 with a 3.12 earned run average. He struck out 125 and walked 103. He completed sixteen games, giving up the lowest number of hits per nine innings in the league and standing second in the league in strike-outs per nine innings.

Still, Vander Meer was disappointed in his season. He believed he could have had a better year if boils in his ears hadn't hospitalized him for a month. "I had seven boils in one ear and six in the other. I lost about 15 pounds. They didn't know much about inside boils at that time, and all I could do was put heat lamps on them."

In addition to Vandy's two no-hitters earning him the *Sporting News*'s Major League Player of the Year Award, he received a handful of other honors. In addition, he was *Baseball Magazine*'s Rookie of the Year. His teammate Frank McCormick was selected as second-best rookie of the year. The magazine's Daniel M.

Daniel said Vander Meer "gave no indication of outstanding genius" in the Minor Leagues. (Did he not know about Vandy's 295 strikeouts at Durham in 1936?) Yet after his performance in 1938, Daniel wrote, Vander Meer "looks like a sure star, one of the greatest freshman pitchers in the history of the major leagues."

In addition to the money he earned in endorsements from his sensational year, Vander Meer's salary jumped from $5,000 to $12,000, including the annuity. The average salary of a Major Leaguer in 1939 was $7,306, so Vander Meer was compensated well for a young player. "That was unheard-of for most third-year players," he said. "You could count on one hand the number of players making twenty-five thousand dollars a year in both leagues."

Joe DiMaggio, not yet in his prime but close, was paid $15,000 in 1937. Twenty-game winner Red Ruffing received the same as DiMaggio, although he had to hold out to get it.

Among Vandy's endorsements was one for Huskies Whole Wheat Flakes in which he and other players, including Bill Terry and Lou Gehrig, agreed that the cereal was "tops in taste . . . and help[s] build muscle, too." Several years later he endorsed Camel cigarettes, sharing an advertisement in *American Legion* magazine and *Collier's* with another pitcher, Gene Bearden. In the ad he tells Bearden, "I've smoked Camels for ten years, Gene. They're mild, and they sure taste great." Bearden replies, "Right, Van. It's Camels for me, too, . . . ever since I made the thirty-day mildness test."

In the *Sporting News*, Vandy was shown rearing back to throw a pitch in a half-page advertisement for Chesterfields. The words "Big League Pleasure" were superimposed over his high kick. The ad called him a "great new star of a great old game." Like many ballplayers of his generation, he was an avid smoker. He smoked one or two packs of cigarettes a day until the day he died. He called cigarettes "my one bad virtue."

Bill McKechnie said he lay awake for hours after the second no-hitter trying to think which pitcher Vander Meer reminded him of. "Remember, all of the truly greats were mighty big guys. Johnny hasn't the long arms of those fellows. His motion, however, reminds me greatly of Watson Clark, the old Brooklyn left-hander [who pitched ten years for the Indians, Dodgers, and Giants]."

Vander Meer received some advice from baseball commissioner Kenesaw Mountain Landis, who grabbed him by the throat of his sports shirt and told him, "Young man, remember two games don't make you. It's over the years that count." And Vandy took it to heart. In truth, he'd always said that the game that gave him confidence that he could pitch in the Major Leagues was that victory over the first-place Giants earlier in the year. "When the last Giant was out, I felt I had arrived as a major leaguer," he said two months after his no-hitters. "Until that game I still was a question mark."

Over the next few months the honors kept rolling in. At a banquet in his hometown attended by 350 people, he was made an honorary deputy sheriff of Passaic County, an honorary police officer of Bergen County, and an honorary policeman of Midland Park. He was given a sapphire ring at the banquet. When Vander Meer thanked the gathering, he added, "I expect the Cincinnati Reds to win the pennant this year and when I pitch in the World Series I'll be a winning pitcher. If we don't win this year, we'll have that flag next season." He couldn't have been more wrong about 1938, but he was right about the following year.

A week after the banquet the Kellogg cereal company announced its All-American team of the "most popular" players in a nationwide voting contest. The voting had nothing to do with performance, just popularity. Vander Meer was among five pitchers. The others were the Yankees' Red Ruffing, the Giants' Carl Hubbell, the Red Sox's Lefty Grove, and the Tigers' Tommy Bridges. Each player received a new car.

The Rest of the Season 16

In his next start, four days after the second no-hitter, the Reds were in Boston, where Cy Young was one of the 34,511 fans who came to see if Vander Meer had any more hitless innings in him. Seventy-year-old Young was especially interested, as he held the record, with twenty-three hitless innings in a row, spread out over several games.

Had it not been for Hank Leiber's bloop single with two outs in the ninth inning of the game before Vandy's first no-hitter, he would have strung together almost thirty innings, far surpassing Young's record.

Would Vandy pitch a third straight no-hitter? The odds were about 172,800,000 to 1 that he would. Vander Meer managed to pitch 3⅓ more hitless innings, running his string to 21⅔ innings. "You could just feel what everybody in the ballpark was thinking: What gives with this guy? To tell you the truth, I was beginning to wonder myself," he said.

"Hey, I was hot that week—on fire," he said. "No one could touch me. I could have had three no-hitters, four. It was just a groove I got in that was perfect."

To face Vander Meer, Boston manager Casey Stengel had a trick up his sleeve. In the fourth inning he switched to first base from coaching third. "Of course, Casey is Casey, and I think he tried to psyche me a little," Vander Meer said.

As Stengel crossed over to first he passed in front of Vander Meer, who was beginning to loosen up. He looked down in an effort to prevent anyone from seeing he was talking to Vander Meer and said, "John, we're not trying to beat you, we're just trying to get a base hit."

Sure enough, Stengel "put the bee on me," Vander Meer said. In this game Stengel played Debs Garms, who sat out the first no-hitter. He smacked a 2-and-1 pitch back through the box, extending his hitting streak of eighteen games. "I'm glad that's over," Vander Meer said. "I only wish the first man up could have [gotten a] hit and ended the strain," he said.

"I was relieved," Vander Meer said, "the pressure had become too much and I was glad to get out from under it. Enough was enough." He was so relieved about the string ending, "I think if I'd have had a ten-dollar bill in my baseball pants I'd have gone over to first base and handed it to Garms." The game was the easiest Vandy had been in all season. The Reds won 14–1. Vander Meer surrendered his lone run in the seventh inning and allowed only four hits in the game.

In a remarkable four-game streak, he pitched thirty-two consecutive innings without giving up a run. In the remaining four innings of the total thirty-six that he pitched, he gave up two runs and seven hits. For June he was 7-0 with a 1.46 earned run average.

Five days after the second no-hitter, a Cincinnati streetcar conductor told a reporter that he wondered whether he had anything to do with Vander Meer's success. In April the conductor had written a letter signed "A Red Rooter" that offered the left-hander tips on how to be a better pitcher.

William Shambaugh did have some credentials for offering the help: he had pitched semipro ball for several years and was on the pitching staff of the Nationals in the John Spinney League. "I figured I knew a little something about the game," he said. "I played a good many years, and I've studied baseball for forty years."

Shambaugh had read that Vandy was having control problems. So he wrote a letter suggesting that Vandy "should just pitch to the catcher, the same as if he were on the sidelines warming up. And I pointed out that if someone does hit the ball that seven men are back of him to get it."

Shambaugh noted that a good hitter gets a hit only once every three at bats. "You see, I wanted him to get to controlling that ball, for I just sensed he was a great pitcher." The conductor doubted that Vander Meer paid him much mind, since he never acknowledged the letter, but "he might have. . . . Anyway, he's the only one who would know."

Shambaugh said he hoped Vander Meer "won't just think I'm another nut. You can't tell, though, he might have taken my advice seriously. Anyway, he's certainly tightened up to become one of the greatest pitchers of all time since then."

Vander Meer apparently never responded to Shambaugh's letter or acknowledged that he had ever received the letter. While the advice might have been on target, certainly a pitcher who had reached the Major Leagues would have employed the techniques Shambaugh was passing along. But Shambaugh's effort showed the admiration and good intentions that his fans— at least this one—had toward Vander Meer. At any rate, Vandy was doing just fine without outside help. He was on a nine-game winning streak, after all.

Meanwhile, sportswriters were drawing comparisons between fellow hard throwers Vander Meer and Bob Feller, the boy wonder of the American League. Giants future Hall of Famer Mel Ott said Vandy was a better pitcher than Feller. Ott played exclusively in the National League and faced Vander Meer more than Feller, although he batted against Feller either in spring training or an All-Star Game. He said Vander Meer had better control than Feller, which seems difficult to believe considering Vandy's wildness—although it does say something about Feller's control.

Vander Meer's fastball was faster, Ott said. "I guess one of them will be about as good as the other as long as both are in the big leagues, but Vandy should last longer. He has a smooth delivery, while Feller's throwing is jerky."

That prediction fell far short. Vander Meer played fourteen seasons, while Feller played twenty years, winning 266 games and losing 162. He was inducted into the Hall of Fame in 1962. Vandy was 119-121 and never came close to the hall.

On the basis of his winning streak and no-hitters, Vander Meer was selected to pitch in that year's All-Star Game in Cincinnati, the sixth All-Star Game in Major League history. The hometown crowd now had even more reason to attend: Giants manager Bill Terry named Vandy his starting pitcher.

Terry could have chosen the great Carl Hubbell, but he called Vander Meer the National League's "best bet. . . . He showed me plenty of stuff when he worked against us, and he ought to be a cinch to fool those American League batters the first time they see him. He's the toughest man in the league to hit against right now." Terry likely also considered the fact that Vandy would be pitching before a hometown crowd.

Vandy was the first rookie pitcher to start an All-Star Game. The Reds' Ival Goodman, Ernie Lombardi, and Frank McCormick also started for the National League.

"It's a wonderful honor for me to be on the team, not to mention the distinction of being the starting pitcher," Vander Meer said. "That was a hard game for me last Sunday [a loss to the Cubs], but I'll be all right, I guess. I know that I'll be in there doing the best I can."

Vandy's mother, father, sister, and brother were there to root him on. More than 143,000 people applied for tickets to see Vander Meer pitch against an American League team that had ten future Hall of Famers. Even though the park could hold slightly more than 26,000, they managed to squeeze in 27,067. Box-seat tickets that cost two dollars were scalped for twenty-five dollars apiece; one broker disclosed that he sold twelve grandstand seats for a whopping one hundred dollars.

Vandy was subjected to some good-natured ribbing by his National League teammates in the clubhouse. Outfielder Earl Averill, a future Hall of Famer, told him, "Hey, Johnny, why don't you just throw the ball straight down the middle. No one will be looking for it." Actually, Vandy said years later, that's exactly the advice Terry had given him, namely that the American League's batters would be looking for Vander Meer to nibble the corners, and firing it down the middle would catch them off guard. "Just pump it in there, John," Terry said.

Vander Meer was in awe. As a twenty-three-year-old rookie he was to face a team of American League All-Stars that included Charlie Gehringer, Jimmy Foxx, Joe DiMaggio, Bill Dickey, Joe Cronin, Lefty Grove, and standout first baseman Lou Gehrig, who had been selected to every All-Star Game since its inception in 1933. With that lineup, the American League was heavily favored to win.

Vandy had pitched against Gehringer, Foxx, and Cronin in exhibition games, "but those others are just strangers. Maybe it's just as well."

While Vandy may have been in awe of the All-Stars he was facing, he rolled through three innings against their powerful lineup, only giving up a hit to Cronin to open the third while striking out one and walking no one in a game won by the National League 4–1.

After the game Vander Meer went around the team's locker room collecting autographs of his teammates. He recalled that because he had to pitch only three innings, "I let everything fly . . . and got the ball over the plate and got done with the ballgame."

American League players raved about Vander Meer's performance. "He's got it," Detroit Tigers catcher Mickey Cochrane said. "He has the poise of a veteran and plenty of stuff." Yankees catcher Bill Dickey agreed. "This Vander Meer is plenty fast and has the hook [curve]. He can't be compared with Lefty Grove when [he] was at the top of his form. But make no mistake, the boy is good." "He's wicked," said DiMaggio. "Johnny will get better as he goes along. He throws with everything he's got and that's plenty. . . . The ball was on me before I could swing."

Vandy recalled years later that the home run total and combined batting average of the American League's lineup was better than any All-Star team in history. "It felt good, real good, beating them, and my good friend Lefty Grove. That's the only game he ever lost in a World Series or All-Star contest." That wasn't true, but it sounded good. Grove lost a World Series game in 1930 while pitching for the Philadelphia Athletics against the St. Louis Cardinals.

In his first year as the Reds' skipper, McKechnie lifted Cincinnati from being a 56-98 team in 1937 to 82-68 in 1938. Ernie Lombardi was the National League's top hitter, and Frank McCormick led the league in hits.

Paul Derringer pitched more complete games and innings while giving up fewer walks than anyone; he also was second in earned run average, wins, and strikeouts. All of this despite the fact that Derringer "loved good food and good whiskey," teammate Billy Werber noted. That became evident years later at team reunions when Derringer, who had ballooned to almost three hundred pounds, couldn't squeeze into his old uniform.

McKechnie saw some potential in the team but also worried about its weaknesses. "You can't tell what a club like this—a young club—will do," he said. "Our boys are overanxious sometimes. We beat ourselves in about half the games we lost. Steady clubs—veteran clubs—don't do that. Then there's another thing. Everybody was talking about us having four men up among the five leading hitters. I'll bet we're leading the league way off in men left on bases—must be leading by a hundred. . . . We haven't a great team, but we have the makings of a great team—maybe."

There's nothing like a winning team and optimism about winning a pennant to help boost attendance. Having a new hero in Johnny Vander Meer certainly helped. The Reds picked days when attendance would be highest for him to pitch—five games on Sundays, two at night, and two on Saturdays. Attendance at Cincinnati games jumped 282,013 for the 1938 season, the biggest increase in either league. The Reds drew 732,013. Only two teams topped the one million mark—the Cubs and the Yankees.

Based on Vander Meer's two no-hitters and nine-game winning streak, the Reds looked to him as the answer to their prayers of bringing a World Series to Cincinnati. But with a couple of exceptions, Vandy never lived up to his promise. Injuries, military service, and illnesses hampered his effectiveness. For the rest of Vandy's career, he was never more than a mediocre pitcher. Yet the Reds stuck with him through twelve seasons in the hope that the magic he performed in that two-game stretch would return. Would they have been so patient with any other hurler?

17 A New Season

> Now listen, young fans, and you shall hear
> Of a fireball pitcher named Vander Meer;
> He threw no-hitters, two in a row,
> And then he ran into all sorts of woe.
>
> **JACK NEWCOMBE**, *The Fireballers*

As Vander Meer approached spring training in 1939, he told reporters, "I am not a big league pitcher yet. . . . I have to learn to control my wildness. Control is the most important pitching attribute. A blinding fastball or a fast-breaking curve doesn't mean a thing if you can't signal your catcher the exact spot it's going to strike his glove."

A reporter asked him if he expected to throw another no-hitter. "Well, you never can tell," he said. "I didn't expect to throw that no-hit game against Boston, nor the next one against Brooklyn. It's all luck."

Cincinnati fans in 1939 were looking for a pennant. They needed something to keep their minds off a world on the brink of another war, and the Reds' pennant chances gave them that diversion.

The Reds had won only two pennants in their history, in 1882 and 1919. The team's 1919 World Series win was tainted by the Black Sox scandal, in which eight Chicago White Sox players were accused of throwing games, essentially giving the series to the Reds. McKechnie was cautious about the Reds' pennant chances. "Ask me next August," he told sportswriters. "Some of the new boys were all right in the minors, but that isn't in the majors." Measuring his words carefully, he said, "Yes, we don't know just what to expect from the youngsters. We have a couple . . . boys [coming up from the Minors who might help]." Beyond that he wouldn't say much.

Sportswriters said the pennant race would come down to four teams—the Reds, Giants, Cubs, and Pirates. Cincinnati, they said, had a solid pitching staff, with Paul Derringer, Bucky Walters, Whitey Moore, Lee Grissom, Eugene "Junior" Thompson, and Vander Meer.

Sadly, the Reds came to learn they couldn't count on Vander Meer. If he was living a dream in 1938, the next year was a nightmare. He became sick that spring with a recurrence of his stomach troubles and missed most of spring training. He lost fourteen pounds over nine days in the hospital. When the team headed north for the start of the season, Vandy remained behind to work himself into shape. He managed to return to Cincinnati in time to pitch opening day, but he might have tried to catch up too fast, because he hurt his shoulder.

Vander Meer seemed to have lost his stride and his confidence. He got off to a poor start. He was wild as usual, walking sixty-nine batters in eighty-four innings—an unacceptable ratio to McKechnie.

Surprisingly, Vander Meer was picked to join the National League All-Stars for their game against American League counterparts on July 13, 1939. He was one of seven Reds selected by National League managers. The pick must have been one of sentiment for his two no-hitters and his performance in the 1938 All-Star Game. Certainly his record in 1939 was undeserving. His own manager didn't pull him out of the bullpen until the middle of the season.

Shirley Povich, the esteemed baseball writer for the *Washington Post*, said Vander Meer "has lost his magic this season and is not regarded as a solid risk." He didn't play in the All-Star

Game, won by the Americans 3–1 before 62,982 in Yankee Stadium, joining the ranks of five other National League pitchers who didn't take the mound.

The Reds looked like the team to beat in the National League when, on May 16, they went on a twelve-game winning streak. They took over first place in the National League at the end of the streak by winning three out of four from the Cardinals. Then they held on to first the rest of the season, finishing 97-57—four and a half games ahead of the Cardinals. The pitching staff racked up an ERA of 3.05, their defense had a .981 fielding percentage, and they ranked lowest in errors in the National League with 117.

Vander Meer, however, offered minimal help. While he still could pitch, he needed more rest between starts, which cut down on his efficiency. McKechnie remained confident, though, saying, "I still think Vander Meer will be a great pitcher one of these days."

In mid-August Vandy began once again to search for the cause of his "old bugaboo," wildness. The Reds trained a motion-picture camera on him from the first baseline to get a better look at what could be provoking his problem.

They discovered that he was releasing the ball too soon on his follow-through and began working on correcting that. But he didn't improve much and ended the year with a 5-9 record and a 4.67 earned run average. He started twenty-one games and pitched 129 innings, striking out 102 and walking 95 batters—a poor performance compared to the previous season when he pitched 225 innings and walked 103.

The Reds faced the Yankees, who had run up a 106-45 regular season record, in the World Series. The Yankees had won the three previous World Series, a feat the team repeated in 1939 with a sweep of the Reds. All Vander Meer could do was sit and watch. He didn't pitch an inning. "The World Series came just one year too late for me," he said.

In November Vandy could hardly wait for spring training to

roll around. "I've put my regrets of 1939 behind me," he said. "I know I had a bad year. What's the use of offering any alibis, but I think I'll be all right again next summer. I never said anything about it during the season, but I believe my trouble last year was due to an old back injury."

In December Vander Meer went from the top to the flop. He had the dubious distinction of sharing the most resounding flop of 1939 with the Northwestern football team, which expected to contend for the Big Ten title but lost five of eight, four by shutouts. Not only that, sportswriters singled out the Reds as the third-biggest disappointment of the year thanks to the World Series sweep.

In 1940 the Reds again were favored to finish atop the National League. An optimistic Bill McKechnie, when asked about the team's chances of beating out the Cardinals, said, "In March, yes, they can have it, but in September we'll take it again. What's all this about the Cardinals? We won the pennant last year by beating that club. And we have a better club this year."

The Reds did have a solid pitching staff. Although McKechnie wasn't counting on Vander Meer to step in, he wasn't giving up hope. "His arm is all right," McKechnie said. "Yes, sir, his arm is all right. He can wheel the ball in there just as he did before his arm went bad." Reporters asked if Vander Meer had lost confidence. "I don't know," the manager said. "You see, he had a lot of hard luck and maybe it shook his confidence. I'm pretty sure he has his stuff back again, but he'll need confidence to put it over."

Vandy knew he needed to get back in favor with McKechnie and to regain his confidence. As he headed to spring training in Tampa, Florida, he said, "I'm going down there as a 'busher.' I'm just trying to prove to Bill McKechnie that I have the stuff. And I'm sure that I can make the grade."

In March the Reds took a ship to Havana to play a Cuban team led by legendary manager Adolfo Luque for a six-thousand-dollar guarantee. McKechnie called on Vander Meer to pitch the first game. The Cubans pounded Vandy, who gave up a grand slam home run to Alejandro Crespo. The Reds lost 11–7, ending the series with one win, one loss, and one tie.

Writers noted that Vandy gave up eight base on balls during three innings of spring training. "Five in one inning," McKechnie said. "Maybe that was my mistake. Maybe I should have had him out of there when I saw he was going wild. But I wanted to give him a chance to fight his own way out. I thought that would build up his self-confidence."

By the end of spring training Vander Meer's teammates had lost confidence in him. Vander Meer, too, was down on his own ability. "I still got a uniform," he said, "but that's about all." One anonymous player grumbled, "If they could get him out of this league and send him to some minor league club where he could win consistently it might restore his mental equilibrium. But the way he is now, he sweats over every pitch. He works himself into such a lather. His eyeballs fairly pop out of his head with the exertion of a throw. It's too bad. He's a fine boy. But I doubt he has the stuff he had in 1938. He didn't have all of it last year."

Sportswriters speculated that it wasn't enough to have a strong arm. In addition to being wild, they said, Vander Meer was not a student of the game. They also questioned whether his various illnesses and sore arm were, in fact, real.

If everyone around Vandy was losing confidence in him, General Manager Warren Giles was not. "He came back once," he said, "and right now we refuse to believe he can't again." Nor was McKechnie, who said, "He still has as much stuff as ever, his arm was never better and I think he's coming along toward winning."

Lombardi also came to his defense. "Johnny has no reason for being a failure this year. He merely must get over being afraid to turn the ball loose with all his speed. In his last two times out, he showed improvement in his control and also pitched with freedom. I believe he's coming back to his 1938 form." But Vander Meer wasn't much help to the Reds in 1940. The press wondered why his pitching had dropped off so dramatically after his dual no-hitters. Was it a jinx?

"There's no such thing as a no-hit jinx," he said. "My no-hit games were good luck. I think that I'll be winning games from now on," he said in the midyear. "I twisted something in my back while pitching a year ago. I'm all right now. For a while, I could throw a fastball, but when I went to throw a curve I'd almost faint."

Nonetheless, Vander Meer appeared in only ten games that year before spending time with the Indianapolis farm team. McKechnie had suggested that Vandy go to Indianapolis to work on getting his confidence back. He couldn't afford to take a chance with Vander Meer's inconsistency. If Vander Meer were sitting on the bench he would have little opportunity to work on his wildness during a pennant race. McKechnie was hoping the left-hander would fine-tune his game in Indianapolis to help the Reds down the stretch drive.

Before going to Indianapolis, Vandy had to clear waivers, which meant that any team could pick him up. None did. No one wanted a pitcher with a sore arm, not even one named Double No-Hit Johnny.

"I realize the only way I can help myself and the club," Vandy said, "is to get better control. With the Reds in first place manager McKechnie feels he can't take a chance with me. Therefore, I'm glad of the opportunity to get regular work, and as soon as I get four or five good games under my belt I expect to be back."

Giles agreed with the decision. He told Vander Meer that Indianapolis manager Jewel Ens would work with him on his control. Some of his teammates weren't unhappy to see him go. As third baseman Bill Werber tells it, some of the players were cool toward Vander Meer because he failed to share credit with them after his two no-hitters despite having a strong defense behind him. Moreover, his teammates didn't want him to take the mound. Their morale fell when he pitched.

Werber also said his teammates thought Vandy was a cheapskate. He would, for example, ride in a cab with his teammates and then contend that all he had was a fifty-dollar bill, letting the other players pay the fare and then never reimbursing them. McKechnie, obviously having heard about this, gave Vandy some advice when he went down to Indianapolis: "John, when you ride in a cab, cover the fare. When you go to the movie, pay the way. I'll be checking with Jewel from time to time and if your progress is good I'll bring you back up."

In his first game with Indianapolis Vander Meer won 5–3 with a six-hitter. He walked three and struck out ten in the seven-inning nightcap of a doubleheader.

After he saw a specialist, Vander Meer's shoulder injury began to heal. "Boy, I sure am ready now," he said. "I know I've helped myself by coming here, and I sure hope I've helped Indianapolis a little in return. I'm for the Reds all the way and I'll do anything they say—stay here as long as they want me to, but I'd sure like to get back to the big time."

During a stretch in Indianapolis when he was 6-2, Vander Meer remarked, "My arm is freer. I'm looser all over and my control is better. Give me a spot on the Reds again and I'll stick."

After winning six and losing four, striking out 109 in 105 innings for an ERA of 2.40, Vander Meer earned a promotion back to the Reds at the end of August. The Reds were fighting down to the wire for the National League pennant. "My going to Indianapolis was the best thing that ever happened to me," Vander Meer recalled. "I got off on the right foot there."

While he was in Indianapolis the Reds began to play better, taking over first place on July 7. They then went on a tear, winning fourteen out of seventeen games and holding on to first place the rest of the year.

By early September, with Vandy back with the Reds, McKechnie grew confident the team would win the pennant. "Johnny Vander Meer is back with us again after being treated in Chattanooga for a kink in his pitching shoulder, and I'm confident he will help us in our September campaign."

The left-hander's first start back with the big club came against Pittsburgh on September 5. The Reds had beaten the Pirates seventeen straight, dating back to the previous season, and had won eleven of their last fourteen games—apparently on the road to recovery after the suicide of their backup catcher Willard Hershberger.

Now it was time to see if Vander Meer really had recovered. He pitched well, but the Reds trailed the Pirates 3–2 going into the eighth inning. Then Cincinnati scored four times, twice behind a single by Frank McCormick, to take the lead 6–3. Vandy retired the Pirates in the ninth for a complete game win. He gave up nine hits, walked five, and struck out six. The win kept the Reds eight games in front in the National League pennant race.

In his next start Vander Meer outlasted his boyhood hero, Carl Hubbell, 5–2. Then, on September 18, the Reds needed only one game to cinch the pennant. Vander Meer got the nod to pitch against Philadelphia in a game he called "my biggest day in baseball." How could that be after pitching back-to-back no-hitters? He said he wasn't as keyed up for those games as he was for a game in the heat of a pennant race. "I felt good after those no-hit, no-run games in '38, but nothing like I felt that afternoon in 1940," he recalled four years later.

His teammates were unhappy with the decision to give such an important game to Vandy when the club's two aces, Paul Derringer and Bucky Walters, were okay to pitch.

The decision apparently came from Warren Giles.

Players questioned whether Giles was trying to help Vander Meer with his endorsements and appearances. "[Vander Meer's] the one he wanted to start the game," pitcher Junior Thompson said. "Giles insisted it be Vander Meer, which the team didn't think was fair. I remember McKechnie getting us all around and telling us it wasn't his idea for Vander Meer to pitch what could have been and wound up being the clincher. That was McKechnie's style though. He never made a move that didn't get us all together to talk about it."

The Reds faced the Phillies' Hugh Mulcahy, a tough, savvy veteran pitcher. Only a little more than two thousand fans were in the Philadelphia stands to watch what became an epic battle.

The Phillies got two runs off Vandy in the second, but the Reds got one back in the fifth. "I began to wonder if I was going to let the team down on the one game it needed to clinch the flag. It was life-and-death in my mind," Vander Meer said. "I had to hang on to my 'comeback.' I had to win."

The Reds tied it in the seventh. In the tenth Cincinnati scored a run, but Vander Meer couldn't hold the lead as the Phillies knotted the score again. "It was true that I had blanked them for seven innings between the second and tenth, and the team was all the time telling me how good I was going, but there it was, we'd been ahead and I'd let the Phillies tie us."

Vandy shut Philadelphia down in the eleventh and twelfth. "I was still pumping it at the end of [twelve] innings and my arm was real strong," he said. "So that was great satisfaction that my arm was all right again."

Then he came to the plate in the thirteenth. What manager today would have let a pitcher bat after pitching twelve innings and leading off the thirteenth? Mulcahy was still in the game as well. Vander Meer, an average hitter for a pitcher who had gotten a hit in each of his back-to-back no-hitters, lined a hit into left center and legged it into a double. He said he "ran faster than I ever had before, I suppose." Then the Reds sacrificed him to third. Frank McCormick beat out an infield single, but Vander Meer had to hold at third.

The next batter, Ival Goodman, hit the ball hard twice and Vander Meer raced home, but both balls were foul. Then Goodman hit a short fly ball. McKechnie, who was coaching third base as managers did in those days, told Vandy to tag up and "run,

Johnny, run." When the ball settled into the outfielder's glove, Vander Meer took off for home "in the hardest slide I ever made and looked up through the dust." He was safe.

With the Reds ahead, McKechnie, who worried that all that running had tired Vander Meer out, pulled the pitcher for Joe Beggs, who retired the side. The Reds were the National League champions.

The team's worries had been for naught. Vandy had struck out ten and walked five. Just as important to him as cinching the pennant was the fact that his confidence had been restored. "I knew I hadn't done any permanent damage to my arm," he said, "and was going to be able to continue playing ball.

"What tickled me was I was throwing just as hard in the thirteenth as the first inning and I wasn't tired," he said. "I knew my arm was back and that I had a future ahead."

"I'm glad it's all over," said a jubilant McKechnie. "Now we can go ahead and prepare for the World Series, something we were unable to do last year. We'll take it easy for a day or two and then start getting ready."

Vandy appeared to be back in form, although his statistics for the year were not overwhelming. He won three games and lost one with an ERA of 3.75. He had started only seven games and pitched forty-eight innings. His forty-one walks matched the number of his strikeouts.

The Reds finished twelve games ahead of the Dodgers with a record of 100-53. By winning the pennant after being swept in the 1939 World Series, the Reds overcame an old baseball axiom: a team that lost four straight games in the World Series would not get another shot at the series the following year.

The Reds faced the Detroit Tigers in the World Series. The potent Tigers, with future Hall of Famers Hank Greenberg and Charlie Gehringer, were favored to win. They also had good pitching, with Bobo Newsom winning twenty-one games and losing three while Schoolboy Rowe was 16-3.

The National League was considered inferior to the American League, as the NL had not won a championship since 1934.

The Reds surprised the critics, winning the last two at home and beating the Tigers 4–3.

Vander Meer was supposed to pitch in the crucial fifth game of the series, but twenty minutes before it started McKechnie switched to Junior Thompson without explanation. Vandy was disappointed because he was over his arm trouble and thought he could do the job. "I was back . . . in my stride. So I was a little upset about it." But he didn't say anything to McKechnie.

Thompson was knocked out early, giving up six runs in 3⅓ innings. Vandy got into the game in the fifth inning and pitched three innings of shutout ball in a mop-up role. The Reds lost 8–0.

When the money for winning the World Series was split up, Vander Meer's teammates voted to give him only $1,000. They thought he hadn't contributed enough in the past two seasons to deserve more.

Thompson said years later that Vander Meer wasn't given a full share because his teammates were still upset that Giles had ordered McKechnie to start Vander Meer in the pennant-clinching game. "That's why Johnny wasn't voted a [full] share," he said. That, and the fact that he didn't pitch much that year.

Baseball commissioner Kenesaw Mountain Landis ordered the players to give him a full share, worth $5,782. "This guy threw back-to-back no-hitters," he said. That certainly didn't endear Vander Meer to his already jealous teammates.

Vandy Bounces Back **18**

McKechnie considered Vandy a key to the Reds' repeating their world championship as 1941 spring training opened. The manager believed Vander Meer was back to his old form and would complement the Reds' four other starters, Derringer, Walters, Thompson, and Turner.

McKechnie apparently felt obligated to explain Vander Meer's slump. Pointing to his own right shoulder, McKechnie said, "Something went on up in here and Johnny couldn't throw at all. He lost all of his rhythm and smoothness. He got to pressing and went from bad to worse. I guess the trouble was both mental and physical." McKechnie added that Vandy had been an effective pitcher the previous season, winning three out of four after he returned from the Indianapolis farm team.

As for himself, Vander Meer said he felt fine and that his confidence had returned. "Last year I just couldn't throw right. My arm hurt and I was tight. You know how it is if you try to walk on a sore leg. You favor it. Well, I was favoring my arm and you can't pitch that way. It's fine now." And he did bounce back. He finished with a 16-13 record and a 2.82 ERA, fourth best in the National League. He also led the league in strikeouts with 202, becoming the National League's first left-handed pitcher in thirty years to strike out more than two hundred batters in a season. His strikeout ratio per game was 8.03, compared with Bob Feller's 6.82. He pitched 226 innings that season, more than in any previous year of his career.

But the season wasn't going as planned for the Reds. They started off poorly and didn't reach .500 until June 9, when

Vander Meer pitched a one-hit 7–0 win over the Phillies. "It was the best game he ever pitched," catcher Ernie Lombardi said. Except for a disputed scratch hit, Vander Meer would have had his third no-hitter.

With the one-hitter, Vandy helped the Reds win eight of their last ten, climbed back to a game and a half out of third place, and took three straight from the Dodgers. Vander Meer's efforts helped earn back the shaky confidence of his teammates, thanks in large part to his hugely improved pitching.

By mid-July Vander Meer had tossed three shutouts, giving up only ten earned runs in his eight wins. But he had lost nine games so far that season, giving up twenty-nine earned runs. He was leading the league in strikeouts with 117 and had an earned run average of 3.12. So to what did he attribute his success? "I'm just getting [the ball] over," Vander Meer said.

On August 20 Vandy was half of a pitching duo that accomplished a rare feat in a doubleheader against the Philadelphia Phillies. He and Elmer Riddle threw back-to-back shutouts, Vandy winning 2–0 and Riddle 3–0. That feat had been accomplished only thirty-nine times in the American League and fifty-eight in the National League since 1890.

On September 6 Vander Meer threw a 2–0 two-hitter at the Cardinals, dropping them two games behind the Dodgers. A single in the first and a double in the fifth were the only hits St. Louis mustered. Vander Meer struck out fourteen, three short of the National League record. McKechnie called Vandy's pitching against the Cardinals the greatest performance of his career, as the left-hander continued to show more poise and more polish.

But the Reds couldn't catch the Dodgers and finished in third place, twelve games back with a record of 88-66.

Vander Meer's career statistics to that date closely matched Lefty Grove's at the same point in his career. The parallels were so close that people were expecting Vander Meer to eventually join Grove in the Hall of Fame.

In his first three seasons, Grove won 43 and lost 38, while

Vander Meer in his first five was 42-39. Before retiring in 1941 Grove won 300 games and lost 141 in his seventeen-year career. Vandy never came close to that record.

After the 1941 season Vandy finished second in the Associated Press poll for comeback player of the year. He finished behind golfer Craig Wood, who had won the Masters.

During the winter the Reds entertained a number of requests to trade Vander Meer. One came from Dodgers general manager Larry MacPhail, who needed a left-handed pitcher. The Reds wanted outfield Pete Reiser, who had hit .343 in his first full year with the Dodgers. But they couldn't reach a deal. McKechnie said it would take a player of Reiser's caliber to pry Vandy loose.

The Reds sought the Pirates' Arky Vaughn, a veteran shortstop, during the winter meetings of baseball executives, but manager Frankie Frisch wanted one of McKechnie's top four pitchers. Vander Meer was one of them.

McKechnie rejected any trade of his pitchers. "No club is in a position to give as much for Vander Meer as we would have to get to part with him," he said. "So he will stay with the Reds. I don't blame some other clubs for wanting Johnny. But they won't get him." McKechnie still had hope that Vander Meer would turn into another Lefty Grove. Vandy headed to Tampa for spring training determined to get into great shape. After his improved years, the Reds were singing his praises. Reds publicist Gabe Paul said that Vander Meer "is considered as potentially one of the greatest pitchers of all time."

There it was again: potentially. While Vander Meer never lived up to that potential, the word stuck with him until he entered military service in World War II.

In a news release, Paul stated that Vandy was a better pitcher in 1941 than he was in 1938 "because he had poise and, while not as spectacular, was much more of a polished performer."

Vander Meer still had control problems, but he wasn't too worried about it. He used his wildness to his advantage. He fell back on his long-used explanation that "it's in a pitcher's favor to have a reputation of being wild. Batters show more respect for the wild man and are careful about crowding the plate and taking toe holds when they know the fellow doing the pitching is apt to let fly with an unintentional wild one. No, I don't want to be a guy who throws nothing except strikes. I just want to eliminate most of it without sacrificing too much of my natural speed. I made a lot of progress in that direction last year and expect to make more this year."

A little wildness, he said, was good, "so I'd just as soon be what the boys call 'pleasingly wild.'" A more accurate statement might have been that he'd be a better pitcher if he could throw "wild" pitches on purpose and pinpoint those he wanted to throw for strikes.

Although he still lacked control, Vander Meer improved in 1942, reducing his walks to 102 compared with 126 the previous year despite starting three more games (thirty-six). At the same time his strikeouts dropped from 202 in 1941 to 186 in 1942. He also had his career-best 2.43 ERA in 1942, the fourth best in the league. He was fifth in the league in innings pitched and complete games. His won-lost record was also the best of his career at 18-12.

Vander Meer was becoming more of a pitcher than a thrower, no longer rearing back and throwing every pitch as hard as he could—although he could still pop them when needed. With an 8-6 record, he was selected to play in the 1942 All-Star Game, the first played since the United States entered the war.

When Vandy got into the game in the fourth inning his first pitch to Joe Gordon sailed high and wide over catcher Walker Cooper's head. It looked like a wild night for the left-hander. But after running the count to 3-2 on Joe Gordon and Rudy York, he struck both out. He pitched three innings, giving up two hits and no runs and striking out four. The American League won 3–1.

The Reds had a horrible August, winning only eleven of thirty games. It would have been worse had not Vander Meer won six of those games while losing only one. He pitched 52⅓ innings and gave up thirteen runs while striking out forty-two. He walked only nineteen. That strong outing in August gave the Reds hope that Vandy would follow the career path of Lefty Grove, who became a solid pitcher at twenty-seven, the same age as Vander Meer.

The Reds finished 1942 76-76, twenty-nine games behind the Cardinals—their worst year since McKechnie took over.

The war years decimated the Reds' lineup, as it did other teams. But Cincinnati's hopes stayed high for the 1943 season. Vandy again made the All-Star team, his fourth selection. He acquitted himself handsomely as he struck out six of the eight American League batters. By striking out six, he tied the All-Star Game record set by his boyhood hero, Carl Hubbell, in 1934. He seemed to pitch best when the pressure was on to succeed against the best. He gave up two hits and one run in 2⅔ innings in the American League's 5–3 win. The game was broadcast throughout the world to America's servicemen.

In 1943 Vander Meer and Riddle matched their 1941 feat with another doubleheader in which they blanked their opponents, this time the Boston Braves on September 26. Riddle won the first game, this time 2–0, and Vander Meer the second, 1–0— only the second time ever that the same two pitchers accomplished this feat.

Vandy had the number of Stan Musial, the Cardinals' future Hall of Famer. In three games against Vander Meer, Musial was hitless. In fact, he hit only .235 against Reds' pitching during a season when he was batting .351. "Vander Meer is one swell pitcher," Musial said. "He has great stuff and is just wild enough at times to keep you loose. Maybe I'll catch up with him yet."

An oddity came to Vander Meer in a September 23, 1943, game against the Giants when he stole home in a double steal. It was the only base Vandy stole in his Major League career.

Thirty-seven pitchers have stolen home since 1900, including Babe Ruth. The last time it was done was in 2001 by the Dodgers' Darren Dreifort.

Cincinnati ended the year vastly improved over the previous season with an 87-67 record that put the team eighteen games out of first place. Vander Meer finished with fifteen wins and sixteen losses. He completed twenty-one of the thirty-six games he started and recorded a 3.34 earned run average. He led the league in strikeouts with 174 and in base on balls with 161.

It was not unusual for hard throwers like Vander Meer to lead the league in walks and strikeouts in the same season. Nolan Ryan did it at least seven times. Bob Feller accomplished the feat four times.

Vandy won more games (forty-nine) than any left-handed pitcher from 1941 to 1943 and led the National League in strikeouts. He lost forty-one games during the same period, in part because of his lack of control. In each of those three years, he finished first or second in walks. Walks led to his downfall in games, not just hits. He allowed opposing batters to hit .214 in 1941 and .208 in 1942.

The War and Beyond 19

Vander Meer pitched in 1942 and 1943 because he was considered physically unfit to serve in the military, but that didn't last long. Feeling better following a bout with colitis after the '43 season, he expected to be drafted despite being married with a three-year-old daughter.

In late January 1944 Vander Meer was called to a New York hospital to undergo an examination for colitis. Doctors found that his health had improved enough for him to be accepted by the navy, and he would be called to duty within ninety days. Thus Vander Meer became 1 of 394 Major League players, or 90 percent of big leaguers, to be drafted.

His induction into the navy took place March 3, 1944. Vandy was twenty-nine years old. He should have been at the height of his baseball career. Like other servicemen who had played professional baseball, he had to wonder if his career was over.

Vander Meer's time in the service proved to be mostly ceremonial. He saw no action on the front lines, instead spending his entire military service entertaining troops by playing baseball, as did hundreds of other ballplayers. He said he'd rather be pitching for the Reds. "But the thing I wanted most was to get into this thing [the war]," he said. "Everyone else was putting on a uniform and I didn't see why I should be an exception." The navy discharged Vandy on December 20, 1945, four months after Japan formally surrendered. All he wanted to do was return to his family and baseball—to his normal life.

With the war over, record crowds were expected to file into Major League parks to welcome back the boys who had served their country. Fans knew that the caliber of baseball would improve with the likes of Bob Feller, Ted Williams, Joe DiMaggio, and Johnny Vander Meer returning to the field.

But Vandy ran into trouble adjusting physically to civilian life after returning home. He said it took him "another year to get back in shape. We had to build up our stamina again. It was the same thing with our coordination." At spring training in Tampa he ran five miles a day. "You only go as far as your legs take you," he said.

Competition proved to be stiff at spring training. Few familiar faces were on hand. The only pitcher Vander Meer knew was reliever Joe Beggs. Several fresh-faced youngsters were trying to earn their way onto the roster. Under the GI Bill every returning serviceman had first rights to his old job, even ballplayers. The training camps were loaded with players, many who hadn't served during the war as well as those who were returning.

Cincinnati was far from the powerhouse team it had been when the war started, and not much was expected from the Reds that year. The prediction riled General Manager Warren Giles. He objected to prognostications of a last-place finish and lashed out, arguing that no one could tell how any team would do after the disruption of the war. "But I know this," he said, "our team is a hell of a lot better than a lot of persons think."

If the exhibition season was any indication, the Reds would be no more than average. They won twenty and lost twenty-two games.

One bright spot during the season for Vander Meer was that he pitched in the longest scoreless game in Major League history that September, fifteen innings of a nineteen-inning game in Brooklyn. He gave up seven hits, struck out fourteen, and walked only two.

Dodgers general manager Branch Rickey called Vandy's stint "the best pitching performance I have ever seen. I know to what weaknesses Vander Meer was trying to pitch, and to see him hit those spots consistently with as much stuff as he had was wonderful."

The Reds started slowly and didn't improve much as 1946 went along. On September 22 Bill McKechnie resigned. He had been the most successful manager in Reds history.

"In the years after the war," Vander Meer said, "the Reds were a pretty good Triple A ball club. The players all tried and did their best. It just wasn't good enough. We didn't have the horses."

The Reds finished in sixth place with a 67-87 record; Vandy won ten and lost twelve with a 3.18 ERA. While the pitching staff was very good, the team had no offense. Vander Meer started twenty-five games and completed eleven. He struck out ninety-four and walked seventy-eight while pitching five shutouts. That was a pretty good record for a team that finished with such a poor record.

When Vandy arrived for spring training in 1947 he encountered only the third Major League manager he ever played for. Johnny Neun was virtually unknown, a Minor League manager who had been in the Yankees farm system, managing fourteen games as interim manager during the 1946 season.

In an interview with a *Cincinnati Times-Star* sportswriter during spring training, Vander Meer said that although it would be nice to pitch another no-hitter, "it's the least of my worries. I'll take victories and somebody else can have the no-hitters. I've lost a little of my speed, but I've got a better curve ball than I used to have."

Later in the year he told another reporter that he longed for his fastball. "The truth of the matter is I can burn them in sometimes, but I get along mainly on control. That's pretty funny because I used to be plenty wild."

The Reds had a potent pitching staff but not much else. Vander Meer was joined by Ewell "The Whip" Blackwell, Bucky Walters, and Ken Raffensberger. Blackwell led the league with twenty-two wins, twenty-three completions, and 193 strikeouts. By 1947, according to Reds outfielder Frank Baumholtz, Vander Meer was just an average pitcher. "He had been around a long time. He was a fine, fine guy. He worked hard and threw hard, and wasn't allergic to hitting somebody."

The Reds played .500 ball until July 4, and then they tailed off, finishing in fifth place with a 73-81 record, twenty-one games behind the Dodgers. That same year Jackie Robinson broke the color barrier. Vandy ended 1947 with a 9-14 record with nine complete games. He walked more than he struck out—87-79—with an ERA of 4.11. During the off-season rumors spread that the Giants were willing to trade Bobby Thomson or Whitey Lockman to the Reds for Vander Meer. Vander Meer wasn't against a trade to the Giants; he had long wanted to pitch in the Polo Grounds so he could be closer to his New Jersey home. The trade never happened. But had it done so, it might have changed baseball history. Three years later Thomson hit "the shot heard round the world," the home run that beat the Dodgers in a pennant playoff game.

Doubts circulated about Vander Meer's return to the Reds at the start of spring training in 1948. The Giants still coveted him and were offering outfielder Sid Gordon in trade. Again the Reds said no.

Vandy proved to be the ace of the pitching staff that year, when the team ended with a combined ERA of 4.47. Vandy won seventeen games and lost fourteen with an ERA of 3.41. He led the league in walks, with 124, while striking out 120. In one game in April he walked twelve St. Louis batters. The Reds finished the season 64-89 and fired manager Neun, replacing him with Vander Meer's former pitching teammate Bucky Walters.

On June 12, 1948, ten years and a day after his first no-hitter, Vander Meer hit the only home run of his career. Walters had told Vander Meer earlier in his career when he came in to pinch-run for Walters, "you may run for me, but you'll never hit for me." Walters was a decent hitter as an infielder before he switched to pitching. He told Vander Meer that if he ever hit a home run "I'll leave the ball park and I'll buy the Champagne." After Vandy hit his home run, a shot over the scoreboard, he saw Walters leaving the dugout for the locker room as he was rounding third base. The Reds beat the Braves 3–2. That night Walters bought the bubbly.

By coincidence, that year Vander Meer gave up the only home run that the Cubs' Emil Verban ever hit in his seven-year Major League career. It came on Verban's 2,424th time at bat in his 682nd game, on September 5.

Vander Meer again was the subject of trade talks during the winter. Durocher, now manager of the Giants, wanted to give the Reds infielder Bill Rigney. Cincinnati never pulled the trigger on a deal. Bucky Walters called the proposed trade silly and said he would be run out of the city if he made the trade.

The Reds later discovered they were lucky they didn't make the deal. On January 20 Blackwell had a diseased kidney removed. Doctors said the pitcher could be laid up for an undetermined time.

Nineteen forty-nine was the last year Vandy played for the Reds. He was the only player left from the pennant-winning years of 1939 and 1940. Despite expressed hopes that Vander Meer still would be an effective pitcher, he was used less often and finished with a 5-10 record and an ERA of 4.90, although he pitched three shutouts. The team fared just as poorly, ending the year 62-92.

Vandy's one highlight for the season came during the second game of the year. He beat the Cardinals 5–0, but the real news was that he didn't walk a batter. The *Sporting News* said it was the first time that had happened in Vander Meer's big league career. It headlined the story "Vandy's First Game without a Free Ticket," saying it might have been a better-pitched game than his no-hitters. The trouble was, the *Sporting News* was wrong; it was the second time he had not walked a batter—he had done it against those same Cardinals on May 9, 1942. Nonetheless, it was an impressive performance for a pitcher nearing the end of his career.

The next year the Reds sold thirty-five-year-old Vander Meer for $30,000 to the Chicago Cubs. Manager Frankie Frisch, high on the deal, said, "I think Vandy'll help our club. He'll get every chance to show his ability and we hope he'll turn into a starting pitcher. He was a good pitcher last year, despite his record."

Vander Meer reported to the Cubs' training camp at 191 pounds, 10 under his previous season's weight. "I've been dieting a lot this winter," Vandy said. "But an injury last spring handicapped me more than any extra weight I might have had. I stepped in a hole and hurt my back in an exhibition in Mobile [Alabama]. I didn't feel right again until August. I made the mistake of trying to pitch when I should have been resting." But his pitching never came around. Again plagued with a sore arm, he finished the year 3-4 in thirty-two appearances.

In 1951 he spent a month with the Cubs at spring training in Arizona. The team released him before the season started.

No doubt Vandy's career was on the downside, but he didn't help himself by angering Frisch. When the hot-tempered manager found Vandy lounging in the sun rather than running several conditioning laps around the ballpark as he had been told to do, Frisch ordered Vander Meer to turn in his uniform. "I don't want any lackadaisical players on my club," he said.

Vander Meer apparently had stripped off the top of his uniform and was sunning himself on a balmy, seventy-five-degree day in front of the right-field bleachers. Another report said that Vandy never got into shape, even after a month of spring training.

Frisch told sports columnist Dan Daniel of the *New York World-Telegram* that the "stakes come too high these days for a club to carry a disinterested player. I did not like Johnny's spirit, and

I told Wid Mathews [the Cubs' director of personnel] that if the club expected me to get anywhere with these kids of ours, Vander Meer would have to go. Well, he's gone, and that's that."

Mathews, in a backhanded reference to Vander Meer, said, "I have an old-fashioned attitude toward baseball. I don't like to see a pitcher spending his off hours reading stock quotations. He might be reading about baseball or he might be talking it. But Wall Street and the diamond just won't jell."

At first Vander Meer refused to comment on the loafing charge. "Baseball has been too good to me for me to start throwing stones," he said. "I believe in the old adage, 'If you can't say something good about a person, just ignore him.'" He said he was in good shape and had been doing a lot of running. "I could outrun any pitcher on the Chicago staff," he said.

Then he said he had been sunning himself on doctor's orders. "A doctor told me to let sun on my back and it would help it. For three days I went out to right field and took my shirt off to get the benefit of the sunrays. Since then look what has happened." In a 1995 interview Vander Meer was asked what he thought of Frisch. Vandy replied tersely, "no comment," then added, "I played too many years for McKechnie."

Vandy wasn't ready to hang up the spikes. He called Cleveland Indians manager Al Lopez about a job as a starter. He knew the Indians could use a left-handed pitcher. "He wanted to know if we'd be interested," Lopez said. "I told him he could work out with us and we'd see what happened." Lopez said he was reluctant to use Vander Meer as a reliever because of his chronic control problems. "If I used him at all it would be in the early innings. I wouldn't use him often to finish games."

The Indians signed thirty-six-year-old Vandy to a contract on April 16, after he pitched three scoreless innings in an exhibition game against the Giants. In his first start in the American League he gave up six runs on eight hits—three of them home runs—in three innings. He surrendered five straight singles in the fourth before he was taken out of the game. It was the only game he appeared in. By June Cleveland had released him. "I guess I just don't have it anymore," he said after the game.

He signed with the Oakland Oaks in the Pacific Coast League. The PCL was a high-quality league. In fact, some PCL players refused to go to the Major Leagues because they were paid more than big league clubs offered. In Vander Meer's first game against league-leading Seattle he struck out ten, giving up seven hits and two runs in 7⅓ innings. He left the game with a pinched nerve in his left elbow. Manager Mel Ott and Oaks owner Brick Laws were pleased with his outing.

"We've had big leaguers come down here and play in a lackadaisical manner," Laws said. "But few have shown the tremendous desire that Vander Meer flashed. He's got crowd appeal. He's an old pro." Vander Meer pitched well but lost several close games. On August 18 he strained a large tendon in his arm after pitching to one batter. His season was over. He'd won only two games and lost six with a 5.14 ERA. As was agreed in his contract with Oakland, he became a free agent after the season. There wasn't much demand, however, for a washed-up, thirty-seven-year-old left-hander.

Over the course of Vander Meer's fourteen-year Major League career he won 119 games and lost 121. He walked 1,132 batters, almost as many as the 1,294 he struck out. He had an unusually high ratio of shutouts to wins by pitching thirty.

Did Vandy wear his arm out? What he did in his career was prodigious by today's standards. He took great pride in finishing games. He started 285 games and completed 131—almost half. Compare that with games finished by the 2007 Cy Young Award winner, C. C. Sabathia of the Cleveland Indians. In the first eight years of Sabathia's career he completed twenty-six games total. That year's runner-up, Josh Beckett, pitched five complete games in eight years. Over the ten-year period from 1995–2004, the height of his career, Pedro Martinez finished 41 games out of 267 started, one of the best complete games records in that period.

In the 1940s Vander Meer completed 103 games, yet he ranked only twelfth in that decade. Hal Newhouser topped the list with 181 complete games. The Major League record holder is Cy Young, who completed 749 games out of 815 started during his twenty-one-year career. Other of Vander Meer's distinguishing statistics:

- 1,132 career walks. The Major League leader is Steve Carlton, with 1,833. Vander Meer ranks eighteenth. Warren Spahn, Tom Glavine, and Fernando Valenzuela had more career walks than Vandy.
- 7.69 base hits for each nine innings, a statistic reserved for pitchers with more than fifteen hundred innings. Nolan Ryan leads, with 6.56. Vandy ranks thirty-first in Major League history.
- .232 career batting average against him. Ryan leads the Major Leagues with a .204 average. Fireballer Bob Feller had a .231 average.
- 162, for most base on balls in a Major League season, set the year he retired. The record is 213 by Ed Seymour of the Giants in 1989.

Years later Vander Meer expressed satisfaction with his Major League career. "No job in the world could have been more enjoyable," he said. "I accomplished something that was of great satisfaction to me. A fellow who can play in the big leagues for ten years or more has the best job ever made."

20 A New Opportunity

In 1951 Vander Meer's financial adviser, Warren Giles, left as the Reds' general manager to become president of the National League. Giles's longtime protégé, Gabe Paul, moved into the general manager's job. One of his first acts was to offer Vandy a two-year contract to pitch and coach in the Minor Leagues. Vandy jumped at the chance, seeing it as an opportunity to someday manage in the big leagues—or, perhaps, to get back to the Majors as a pitcher.

That spring Vander Meer took over as the pitching coach at Tulsa in the Texas League. He also pitched and racked up an 11-10 record with a 2.30 ERA. Among those wins was a no-hitter. It came against a team from Beaumont managed by Harry Craft, the center fielder who caught Leo Durocher's fly ball for the last out of Vander Meer's second no-hitter thirteen years earlier. Five Beaumont players reached base—three on walks, one who was hit by a pitch, and one on an error. A great play by shortstop Alex Grammas, a future Major Leaguer, saved the no-hit game. The attendance was 335.

The next season Vander Meer moved on to Iowa as manager of Burlington on the Three I League, where he again pitched. His team finished in eighth place, and he compiled a 3-4 record with a 3.21 ERA.

Vander Meer said about his experience as a Minor League manager, "A guy has to be part teacher, part player, part father confessor, part road secretary, part telephone operator, and part bus driver." True to his word, he pitched a game on May 26, going the route in a 5–4 loss on an error in the eighth inning.

He took the mound hoping to restore lagging attendance at the ballpark and to set an example for some of his inconsistent starting pitchers.

"Those base-on balls," he said. "I can see now what made my managers gray." After that outing he was so stiff and sore he didn't last an inning in his next start five days later.

From Burlington he moved to Richmond, Virginia, to manage and pitch in the Piedmont League, where he had played in 1936. "I'm tickled to death to get the chance," he said. "The league gave me my break as a player, and I hope it can do the same as a manager." At thirty-nine, he still harbored hope that this opportunity would give him a shot at a Major League managing job, although he knew he'd never return as a pitcher. He said he expected a hustling ball club. "I'm not a fellow who will put up with players who aren't in shape. I don't ask them to do anything I won't do. If I tell them to run, I will run with them. Too many 'good fellow' managers don't last. My players will have to toe the line, or out of town they go."

Before he could get settled in Richmond the club was sold to make room for a Triple A team, and the owner created a new team in Colonial Heights, Virginia, twenty-three miles south of Richmond. In one game Vandy pitched for Colonial Heights, he lost the first game of a doubleheader in relief and then the second game as a starter. Vandy finished the season 1-3 with a 3.86 ERA while his team won sixty-two and lost seventy-eight.

Now concentrating almost exclusively on managing, in 1955 Vander Meer took over the Daytona Beach Islanders of the Florida State League, which kept him closer to his Tampa home. The "old man"—he was forty—was having a good time showing the "kids" how the game was played.

Then, in 1956, Vander Meer led Douglas to the Georgia State League championship. Under pressure from his wife, who wanted to be closer to their Tampa home, Vander Meer moved to Palatka in the Florida State League for two years, where in addition to being the manager he was the bus driver, trainer, and de facto business manager.

"One thing I'm very proud of," Vander Meer said, "is that after twenty years I'm still with the Redleg [*sic*] organization. They've been good to me, and if I had to do it all over again I'd go with Cincinnati again."

The Reds also were happy with him. Warren Giles told Vander Meer's former teammate Bill Werber during a visit in Washington DC that Vander Meer "is far and away the best manager [the Reds have]. He takes these young kids and gives them hours of patient instruction. If they are down on themselves or lonely, he takes them home to dinner. He's like an old mother hen with a brood of young chicks."

The Reds also brought Vandy to spring training each year to work with the rookies. "One thing we know," Gabe Paul said, "among our young pitchers, there has to be respect for the teacher." His double no-hit achievement earned that respect. One pitcher the Reds entrusted to Vander Meer was twenty-year-old Jim O'Toole, who would go on to become one of the starting pitchers on the Reds' all-time team after a ten-year career.

Reds pitcher Joe Nuxhall, who was the youngest player (fifteen years and ten months) to appear in a Major League game in the modern era, recalled Vander Meer's coaching at the Tampa spring training facility. "I remember him coaching us guys, he was strict in the sense of what he thought you should do, but he wouldn't stand around and embarrass you and yell at you," Nuxhall said.

In 1959 Vandy was off again, this time to Topeka, Kansas, in the Three I League, where during his second year he managed a young junior college player who signed a big bonus with the Reds. Vandy helped develop Jim Maloney into an effective Major League pitcher, one who also threw two no-hitters—just not back to back.

Over the winter of 1960 Vander Meer began having trouble making financial ends meet. His jobs were costing him more money than he was making, forcing him to work during the fall and winter in public relations for the Joseph Schlitz Brewing Company. Despite this, he agreed to become manager in

Tampa, where he lived. That cut his expenses because he did not have to move his family during baseball season.

Vander Meer said he liked Class D baseball because travel was kept to a minimum. "I don't enjoy traveling 500 to 600 miles between ballparks like you have to do in the higher classed minors. That's for the younger fellows. I'm getting too old for traveling."

In Tampa he managed Pete Rose, who was in his second year of pro baseball. Rose "was probably the most dedicated player I ever managed or played with," Vander Meer said. "When he would ground to first, he'd run just as fast as if he'd hit a single. If he hit a single, he barreled into second. I always thought he would be a good hitter because he always made contact. He was never that good with the glove at second base because he couldn't go to his right. I wanted to put him at third base or left field."

Vandy asked Rose in the locker room if he always ran to first base like that. Rose replied simply, "I'm looking for a job." To which Vander Meer replied, "Keep running like that and you might get one."

While at Tampa, Vandy also managed future Major Leaguer Lee May, who he persuaded to move from the outfield to first base. Another future star under Vander Meer's tutelage was Jimmy Wynn, later known as the "Toy Cannon," who came to Tampa for a tryout and landed a job.

Wynn called Vander Meer one of the best managers he played under. "He was not only a manager, but he was a father to me. What made him so special was he took me in and I think back to those days, here in Florida, it was tough for a black man, especially for a kid who was nineteen, twenty years old, coming out of college and that's the main reason I respect him a great deal, because of the things he told me to do and how to handle myself, and just go play baseball and he'd take care of everything else." He said when the then–Houston Colt .45s drafted him in the expansion draft, he didn't want to leave Vander Meer. "He is number one in my book and always will be," he said.

In the middle of his second year at Tampa, Vandy was reassigned to Syracuse, a team he had played for on his way up to the Majors. It was a big step for him, one step from the Majors. But at the end of the 1962 season Detroit assumed control of the Syracuse club and brought in its own manager. Because Vander Meer was under contract, he was reassigned as a scout. At that point Vandy decided he was through with baseball. "I enjoyed the hell out of [baseball], but I had to get into the business world," he said.

He accepted a full-time job with Schlitz and stayed fifteen years before retiring at sixty-five in 1979. As military sales manager, Vander Meer covered one hundred military installations in the southeastern United States. "Baseball really did a lot for me," Vander Meer said. "Though you don't sell beer on your name, the military people recognized mine. I did okay financially, so I have a lot to be thankful [for, in] those days."

Vander Meer's name stayed before the baseball-loving public long after he left the game. Virtually every time a pitcher threw a no-hitter, one or more sportswriters would call Vandy to ask him what he thought about the chances of that pitcher throwing a successive no-hitter. He would always answer the question politely and remark that while someone might tie the record it was doubtful anyone would break it.

On the fiftieth anniversary of his no-hitters, Vander Meer went fishing. He wanted to get away from the dozens of telephone calls he expected from reporters who wanted to write about his feat. When the *New York Times*'s Ira Berkow called, his wife, Lois, responded, "Mister, this phone has been ringin' off the wall all week. That's why he went fishing. He just got tired of answering the same questions over and over again. He said he'd just had it. After fifty years, what else can he say about it?"

She told a sportswriter for United Press International who called that day that she had urged her husband to go fishing. "He's been run ragged," she told the sportswriter. "And he does get nervous and jittery with the phone ringing. He's had a bad heart. He has to get away."

He told one reporter who did get through to him, Dwight Chapin of the *San Francisco Chronicle*, the oft-told stories of his baseball years and then told him what he was doing in his retirement years. "I'm a typical Dutchman who loves his flowers," he said. "I stay busy in the yard, do some fishing. And my wife, Lois, and I take boat trips occasionally. I've been all over the place."

Vandy was proud of his accomplishment yet not protective of it. He said it would be good for the game if someone did it again. He did admit to holding his breath whenever a no-hit pitcher took the mound in his next start. "I thought Nolan Ryan and Sandy Koufax had a chance. It'll take somebody like that who throws hard, who can get twelve or fourteen strikeouts. That reduces the number of other outs you have to get."

Vander Meer noted that artificial turf had made it more difficult to pitch no-hitters. "The rug has changed the game," Vander Meer said in 1983. "Lots of balls get through for hits now that would have been outs." On another occasion he said he doubted that anyone would duplicate his feat. "The ball is faster, fences are shorter, and bats are harder," he said. "They are taking it all away from the pitcher and giving it to the batter. As time goes on it will be harder to equal."

On the other hand, he said in 1996, "We didn't have the .225 and .228 hitters you have playing today. . . . Today you have too many players, too many holes in a lineup. Expansion has watered everything down. [Two no-hitters in a row] can be done."

One factor working against pitchers today is media attention. Vander Meer didn't face the pressure today's players do. In fact, the hoopla over night baseball in Brooklyn when Vandy pitched his second no-hitter possibly limited media attention. Also, because no one had ever pitched back-to-back no-hitters before that night, it perhaps kept fans from thinking it could ever happen.

As Vander Meer pointed out, Nolan Ryan had seven chances to pitch back-to-back no-hitters. His seven no-hitters were three more than second-place Sandy Koufax and four more than Bob

Feller. In addition to Feller, two others pitched three no-hitters, and twenty-two hurled two no-hitters. Koufax and Feller each pitched twelve one-hitters. Hall of Famer Steve Carlton pitched six one-hitters but never a no-hitter.

At seventy-three, Vander Meer agreed to participate in a fiftieth anniversary celebration of his first no-hitter at the Astros-Reds game in Cincinnati on June 11, 1988. The Reds showed tapes of his pitching on the scoreboard before he threw out the first pitch. Vander Meer stood about two feet in front of the rubber and threw a hard, high fastball to catcher Terry McGriff as the crowd gave him a standing ovation. Afterward, he signed autographs. "I'll give you a tip on that," he said. "When you can't sign them anymore, you're dead."

In 1991, fifty-three years after his double no-hitters, Vander Meer said it was time for someone else to achieve the feat. "I've had the thing for [fifty-three] years, let somebody else have it," he said. "It's for the good of the game. The game was good for me, so I'd like to be good back to the game. . . . I guess I'm just a big believer that records are made to be broken. That's what baseball is all about."

Vandy had hopes of being voted into the Hall of Fame someday, much as had been the case with three men from the same 1938 team: Lombardi, McKechnie, and MacPhail. But his mediocre career prevented that. What votes he did receive over the years were based solely on that one claim to fame—those consecutive no-hitters. Vander Meer understood that.

Some players believed that one feat should have been enough to include him in the coveted hall.

For example, former Detroit Tiger Hank Greenberg, a Hall of Famer, said Vander Meer deserved special consideration. "I am inclined to say that he should be voted into the Hall of Fame," he said. "First, of course, there is his unique achievement to consider. Then, I think his overall record is good enough and I know he was an outstanding pitcher because I batted against him."

But Hall of Fame rules were against Vander Meer. A section of the rules for admission to the hall reads, "No automatic elections based on performances such as batting average of .400 or more for one year, pitching a perfect game or similar outstanding achievement should be permitted." Seems like the rule was written just for Vander Meer.

"I don't think he should be kept out by some rule," Hall of Famer Yogi Berra said. "Every rule should have an exception and Vander Meer looks like the exception to the Hall of Fame rule." Stan Musial agreed. "I don't like to tell the writers how to vote, but it's hard to argue against a man who performed a feat like that." Casey Stengel agreed. "Sure he does. Two straight no-hitters entitle anyone to the Hall of Fame."

Even sportswriters chimed in. Joe Williams of the *New York World-Telegram and Sun* wrote in 1956 that Vandy deserved to be in the hall. Reflecting the times, he wrote, "That [a double no-hitter] happens about as often as [General Douglas] MacArthur pens a love note to [President] Truman."

There is one consolation: he is featured in the hall's "Great Moments Room," where his jersey, a pen with which he signed his first contract, a photo of him, and an autographed ball are on display.

So how did Vandy stack up against pitchers who are in the Hall of Fame? Fairly well, except in wins and losses. A pitcher with a losing record is unlikely to get into the hall. Vander Meer never pitched for a good ball club except for the 1939 and 1940 pennant winners, when he was injured and pitching poorly. He also lost two years of his career to military service.

Vander Meer's career earned run average was 3.44. Nolan Ryan's was 3.19, Jim Bunning's 3.27, Don Sutton's 3.26, and Bob Feller's 3.25. Vander Meer averaged 139 strikeouts a year, Ryan 245, Bunning 174, Sutton 158, and Feller 166. Vander Meer averaged 226.7 innings pitched a year, Ryan 231.7, Bunning 230, Sutton 234, and Feller 246. Vander Meer completed an average of fourteen games a year, Ryan nine, Bunning nine, Sutton seven, and Feller eighteen. Vander Meer and Feller played in 154-game seasons and Ryan, Bunning, and Sutton in 162-game seasons.

In 1996 Vander Meer returned home to Midland Park to dedicate the Johnny Vander Meer Permanent Exhibit in the Veterans Memorial Library. Nattily dressed in a bright red blazer, looking strong and vibrant, Vandy told the gathering how much growing up in Midland Park had meant to him, especially the friendships he had made and kept throughout the years. "I had a lot of thrills and a lot of fun in my day," he said. "It all started here in Midland Park. Here is where it started and here is where it's going to end."

Eighteen months later, on a clear October 6 in Tampa, Vander Meer, sitting at his kitchen table, asked his grandson to get him a cup of coffee. When Troy Coverdale returned he found his grandfather slumped over, with his face in the *Tampa Tribune*'s sports section. He had died of an abdominal aneurysm at the age of eighty-two. That same day, his longtime friend Dick Jeffer received a letter in the mail that talked about Vander Meer's plans to paint his house and train a new dog.

He was buried holding a baseball in his left hand.

Reds managing executive John Allen called Vander Meer's death "a loss for the organization. His double no-hitter for the Reds always has been and always will be one of the greatest achievements in baseball history."

Asked shortly before he died what he thought history would say about him, Vander Meer said, "History? Hell, all I did was do something no one else has ever done before." And probably never will again.

His double no-hit record "leaves me with the most wonderful memories possible," he said in 1982. "That's great for an old man. I think those two games will make people remember me for a long time."

That's for sure.

Epilogue

The player who came closest to tying Johnny Vander Meer's record was Ewell "The Whip" Blackwell, a lanky right-hander who earned his nickname for the way he whipped the ball to the plate.

Nine years after Vandy's consecutive no-hitters, Blackwell came within two outs in the second game of matching the feat.

Ironically, Blackwell pitched for Cincinnati, too, and his first no-hitter and near no-hitter were against the same two teams Vander Meer beat—Boston and Brooklyn—in the same month and in the same order. One difference was that both of Blackwell's games were pitched in Cincinnati. And who was watching from the Reds' dugout? Vander Meer, of course. Like Vander Meer, Blackwell had no more than an average career, also falling prey to injuries.

Blackwell had an unorthodox pitching style. The right-hander would swing his left leg across his body toward the third-base line and then whip the ball sidearm toward home, giving the batter the impression that the pitch was coming from third base.

"It just came naturally to me," he said. "I threw it about ninety percent of the time."

The pitch was particularly hard for right-handed batters to hit. "I realized my sidearm delivery was intimidating, and I took advantage of it any way I could," he said. "I was a mean pitcher."

Blackwell "pitches like a man falling out of a tree," said Pee Wee Reese, the veteran Dodgers shortstop. Sportswriter Red Smith said Blackwell was so tall and skinny that he "looked like a fly rod with ears."

Blackwell had a career record of eighty-two wins and seventy-eight losses, despite being labeled by the *New York Herald Tribune* as "the greatest young star on the rise in the post-war era of major leagues" and "almost universally acclaimed by National League batters as the best hurler in the circuit."

He was at the top of his game in those two games and he came oh, so close to matching Vander Meer's feat.

Blackwell was in the middle of a sixteen-game winning streak on June 18, 1947, when he threw his first no-hitter, a night game in Cincinnati that the Reds won 6–0 over the Boston Braves. "I wanted to take advantage of those lights," he said. Only one Brave came close to a hit, a line drive by Bama Rowell that Frankie Baumholtz caught against the right-field screen early in the game.

Blackwell had a superstition about not changing his sweatshirt if he was on a winning streak. His teammates chided him about it and kept their distance. But Vander Meer offered Blackwell his encouragement during the no-hitter. "Just keep on sweating, Skinny, and you'll tie my record," he said. "I'm going to try," Blackwell replied.

Nine other pitchers before Blackwell had thrown no-hitters since Vander Meer's feat, but none came close to back-to-back no-no's. Blackwell was the tenth to try. Four days after his first no-hitter, on June 22, 31,204 fans filled Cincinnati's Crosley Field to see if Blackwell could match his teammate's record. The Whip had told a radio show right after pitching the first no-hitter that he was going to repeat his performance in his next start. "Sure, that was a pretty nervy thing to say over the air, but I wasn't talking bigger than I could handle, because there should have been the second no-hitter," Blackwell said. "Didn't miss it by more than an eye blink."

Through the fourth inning neither Blackwell nor his counterpart, Joe Hatten, had given up a base hit. By the sixth Hatten had allowed a hit and walked four men as the Reds took a 1–0 lead. By the top of the ninth the Reds had stretched the lead to 4–0, and Brooklyn still was hitless.

As Blackwell took the mound, Vandy was sitting on the top step of the dugout, waiting to come out and shake Blackwell's hand for tying his record.

Blackwell retired the first batter, Gene Hermanski, a pinch hitter, with a fly ball to Augie Galan in left field. Eddie Stanky, the pesky second baseman known as "The Brat," was up next. Leo Durocher once described Stanky as a player who "can't hit, can't run, can't field but comes to kill you."

Stanky took a ball before hitting a fastball back to Blackwell. He broke his bat on the swing, which distorted the ball's speed. Thanks to his awkward windup and follow-through, Blackwell had trouble getting down for the ball. He said he also misjudged the ball's speed. "I put my knee down and it went right over my leg between the ankle and the calf. I just felt it as it tipped my leg." He added, "I just stood there looking at that ball, that little white ball lying on the grass."

"I'm glad it wasn't called an error because I wouldn't have wanted a no-hitter that way," Blackwell said. "I wasn't the type to get upset, but I was disappointed. I had almost equaled the impossible." Said Vander Meer, "I always thought Blackie should have fielded that ball."

Blackwell got Al Gionfriddo to fly out for what would have been the third out. Up stepped Jackie Robinson, who was in his first year in the big leagues after breaking the color barrier. Robinson looped a single into right field. But then Carl Furillo grounded out to first base. Blackwell ended up with a two-hit, 4–0 shutout.

"It's my own fault I didn't get it," Blackwell said after the game, as sportswriters swarmed him. "I should have fielded Stanky's ball. If I was quicker I would have. And if I got that one, Robinson never would have come to bat, and I would have had my no-hitter. I have only myself to blame."

After the game Vandy told Blackwell, "I was pulling for you

all the way." Blackwell replied, "I know you were," telling Johnny he had seen him on the top step of the dugout waiting to sprint onto the field to offer his congratulations. "And thanks."

The shutout was Blackwell's ninth straight win in a streak that extended to sixteen, all complete games. Five were shutouts. He hung up his glove in 1955 because of a sore arm.

Another pitcher to come close was Howard Ehmke in 1923. On September 7 Ehmke pitched a no-hitter for the Red Sox. Four days later he faced the Yankees. The Yankees' leadoff man, Whitey Witt, topped a pitch in the first inning down the third-base line and beat it out when Howard Shanks fumbled it momentarily. There was no public address system, so no one knew that it was ruled a hit.

Considerable pressure was brought to bear on the official scorer to change his decision and give Shanks an error, but it didn't happen. "If that wasn't an error," said umpire Tommy Connolly, "I never saw one."

So maybe it evened out. Luck certainly had a part in Ehmke's no-hitter. In the seventh inning, the A's Slim Harriss should have had a double, but he missed first base and was ruled out. In the eighth, the official scorer overturned his own ruling that a line drive was an error, not a hit.

Dazzy Vance had a no-hit game with one out in the ninth on September 8, 1925, when Sammy Bohne of the Reds stuck out his bat and dumped a Texas Leaguer into short center field. Five days later Vance pitched a no-hitter, winning 4–1 on a batter who scored after a walk.

The Angels' Nolan Ryan pitched seven innings into his second consecutive no-hitter before he gave up a hit to the Orioles' Mark Belanger in 1973.

In 1952 the Tigers' Virgil Trucks pitched 6⅓ innings of his second consecutive no-hitter when Billy Hitchcock of the A's got a hit.

Houston's Mike Scott threw one no-hitter against San Francisco on September 25, 1986, and six more no-hit innings his next start until the Giants broke his streak at San Francisco. Sixteen years later Scott was asked if he had thought about duplicating Vander Meer's feat. "I didn't even realize the significance of Johnny Vander Meer's until people brought it up after the game," he said.

Cleveland's Dennis Eckersley pitched a no-hitter on May 31, 1977, against the California Angels. He made it through 5⅔ innings of no-hit ball in his next start, on June 3, before giving up a hit to Seattle's Ruppert Jones.

The twenty-two-year-old pitcher did put together the second longest no-hit streak, eclipsing Vander Meer's runner-up spot. Eckersley pitched a 12-inning game, allowing no hits over the last 7⅔ innings. With his 9-inning no-hitter and his 5⅔ innings of no-hits in his next outing, Eckersley pitched 22⅓ innings without a hit. The Major League record at the time was 24⅓ innings by Cy Young. Vander Meer's streak was 21⅔.

The White Sox's Mark Buehrle holds the record for the most batters retired consecutively, set in 2009. While he didn't throw back-to-back no-hitters, during a three-game stretch Buehrle set down forty-five batters in a row. He started the streak by retiring the last batter he faced in the first game, twenty-seven when he pitched a perfect game on July 23, 2009, and then seventeen in a row when he pitched in his next appearance.

The Vancouver Canadians' Tom Drees pitched consecutive no-hitters in May 1989 in the Pacific Coast League, one of which was a seven-inning game. He also pitched another no-hitter that year. Drees played briefly for the Chicago White Sox in 1991, his only trip to the Major Leagues, where he pitched 7⅓ innings and gave up ten hits in four appearances with an ERA of 12.27.

One of the greatest pitching duels, which few fans know about because it was in 1917, was when two pitchers tossed nine-inning no-hitters against each other. On May 2, 1917, the Cubs' Jim "Hippo" Vaughn and Cincinnati's Fred Toney locked up in an epic contest. The two hurlers battled out for out, with Vaughn striking out ten and walking two while Toney got three batters swinging and walked two.

Cincinnati hadn't scored a run in twenty-four innings when they faced the Cubs that day. Reds manager Christy Mathewson decided to put an all-right-handed batting lineup against lefty Vaughn, but it didn't do any good. The Reds hit just one ball out of the infield in nine innings.

"There didn't seem to be very much unusual about the game as it went along," Vaughn said. "I was just taking care of each batter as he came up there, that was all. And I didn't even notice what Toney was doing."

Toney and Vaughn sailed through the ninth inning. "I knew I was tired," Vaughn said, "but I felt that I still had my stuff." And then it all came apart for Vaughn. With one out in the tenth, Larry Kopf hit a single to right. The next batter flied out to center. That brought up "Prince" Hal Chase, who hit a fly ball to right that Larry Williams settled under and dropped. Kopf moved over to third. Jim Thorpe, the famous Indian athlete, then hit a slow roller toward third, and Kopf scored. That ended the Reds' scoring.

In the bottom of the tenth Toney completed his no-hitter, setting the Cubs down in order. When the game was over Vaughn went over to Toney and said, "You've got to pitch the kind of ball you did against me today to beat me from now on, Old Man."

Toney's masterpiece was one of six no-hitters pitched that year, the most in baseball's modern era. Although Vaughn pitched a no-hitter through nine innings, officially he wasn't credited with a no-hitter because he didn't complete the tenth inning.

Another terrific matchup came on September 9, 1965. The Dodgers' Sandy Koufax hooked up with the Cubs' Bob Hendley when the Dodgers were a half game out of first place. Koufax and Hendley threw no-hitters against each other into the seventh inning, even though the Dodgers led 1–0 on a walk, a sacrifice bunt, a stolen base, and an error.

In the seventh Lou Johnson blooped a double down the right-field line. But he didn't score. Hendley didn't give up another hit. Koufax did him one better. Not only did he win 1–0, Koufax threw a perfect game, striking out the last six batters. Koufax finished the year 26-8; Hendley 4-4.

So many so close, but Vandy's record continues to stand alone as one of the most-heralded feats in Major League Baseball history. *Sports Illustrated*'s website in 2006 called Vander Meer's consecutive no-hitters the second least likely record to be broken, ranking behind Cal Ripkin's 2,632 consecutive games. Think about it. To break the record a pitcher would have to throw three consecutive no-hitters. Among the records that *Sports Illustrated* rated behind Vander Meer's were Cy Young's 749 career complete games, Joe DiMaggio's 56-game hitting streak, Nolan Ryan's 5,714 strikeouts, and Rickey Henderson's 1,406 stolen bases.

And the accomplishment takes on added meaning when you consider that at least ten Hall of Fame pitchers never pitched a no-hitter: Lefty Grove, Grover Cleveland Alexander, Robin Roberts, Early Wynn, Red Ruffing, Whitey Ford, Dizzy Dean, Steve Carlton, Don Sutton, and Ferguson Jenkins.

Acknowledgments

No biography could be written without the help of dozens of people who would go unrecognized if authors didn't acknowledge them in their books. So I cannot allow this book to be published without my kudos to the dozens of people who offered tips, conducted research, copied documents, spent time with me on the telephone, critiqued my work, and even listened to countless stories about my protagonist.

There were several remarkable online sources that provided a wealth of information. They include Retrosheet.org, Baseball -almanac.com, The Society of American Baseball Research (Sabr.org), and Baseball-reference.com.

Many thanks to Vander Meer's grandson Troy Coverdale. Also to Ben Harry, Bill Francis, and other staff members of the Baseball Hall of Fame. Marianne Reynolds, Beth Thomas, Steve Kemple, Matt Morris, and David S. Norman of the Cincinnati Public Library sent me copies of newspaper clippings via e-mail. Librarians at the University of Arizona and the Pima County Public Library too numerous to count helped beyond measure.

Eileen Canepari of the Society of American Baseball Research, who provided oral histories of Johnny Vander Meer, Lonny Frey, Bill Werber, and Frank McCormick. Then SABR executive director John Zajc for overseeing an extremely helpful website. My good friend Len Levin found more factual errors in my manuscript than I care to reveal. He also provided me with numerous clippings of Vander Meer's exploits as keeper of SABR archives. Thanks to friends Don Carson, Jim Price, Ron

Navarrette, Jim Boyd, Fernando Acevedo, Roy Smalley, and Wally Sparks for their advice and support.

One who deserves as much credit as anyone is my wife, Marilyn, who is my most worthy critic—and supporter. Her editing saved me from jumbled syntax, grievous grammatical errors, and too many factual errors to keep track of.

I owe a ton of gratitude to University of Nebraska Press sports editor Rob Taylor, who didn't give up on me when I turned in what I now realize was a lousy manuscript. With his guidance, the finished product is a much better effort. And to the anonymous reviewer who plodded through the original manuscript and a revision I owe a great debt of gratitude. He was merciless and right in his critique. His guidance was invaluable.

Finally, many thanks to copyeditor Joy Margheim, whose sharp eye saved me from countless embarrassments in grammar, facts, and messy endnotes and bibliography.

A standing ovation for all of you.

Cincinnati Reds 3, Boston Bees 0
Game played on Saturday, June 11, 1938, (D) at Crosley Field

BOS N	0 0 0		0 0 0		0 0 0		–		0 0 1			
CIN N	0 0 0		1 0 2		0 0 X		–		3 6 0			

BATTING

Boston Bees	AB	R	H	RBI	BB	SO	PO	A
Moore rf	1	0	0	0	1	0	2	0
ˎFletcher 1b	1	0	0	0	0	0	5	0
Mueller ph	1	0	0	0	0	0	0	0
Cooney 1b, rf	3	0	0	0	0	0	4	0
DiMaggio cf	3	0	0	0	0	1	1	0
Cuccinello 2b	2	0	0	0	1	1	1	3
B. Reis lf	3	0	0	0	0	0	3	0
English 3b	2	0	0	0	1	0	0	2
Riddle c	3	0	0	0	0	0	5	0
Warstler ss	2	0	0	0	0	1	3	3
Kahle ph	1	0	0	0	0	0	0	0
MacFayden p	2	0	0	0	0	0	0	0
Maggert ph	1	0	0	0	0	1	0	0
TOTALS	25	0	0	0	3	4	24	8

FIELDING

DP: 1. Cuccinello-Warstler-Cooney.   **E:** Cuccinello (4).

BATTING

Team LOB: 1.

Cincinnati Reds	AB	R	H	RBI	BB	SO	PO	A
Frey 2b	4	0	0	0	0	1	1	2
Berger lf	3	2	1	0	1	0	2	0
Goodman rf	3	0	0	1	0	0	0	0
McCormick 1b	4	0	1	0	0	0	14	1
Lombardi c	4	1	2	2	0	0	5	2
Craft cf	3	0	0	0	0	0	3	0
Riggs 3b	3	0	1	0	0	0	0	5
Myers ss	3	0	0	0	0	2	1	2
Vander Meer p	3	0	1	0	0	1	1	2
TOTALS	30	3	6	3	1	4	27	14

FIELDING

DP: 1. Lombardi-McCormick.

BATTING

3B: Berger (1); Riggs (5).
HR: Lombardi (7).
HBP: Goodman (2).
Team LOB: 5.

PITCHING

Boston Bees	IP	H	R	ER	BB	SO	HR	BFP
MacFayden L(5-2)	8	6	3	3	1	4	1	32

HBP: MacFayden (2).

Cincinnati Reds	IP	H	R	ER	BB	SO	HR	BFP
Vander Meer W(6-2)	9	0	0	0	3	4	0	28

Umpires: HP–George Magerkurth, 1B–Tiny Parker, 3B–Charlie Moran

Time of Game: 1:48   **Attendance:** 5,214

Cincinnati Reds 6, Brooklyn Dodgers 0
Game played on Wednesday, June 15, 1938, (N) at Ebbets Field

CIN N	0 0 4	0 0 1	1 0 0	–	6 11 0
BRO N	0 0 0	0 0 0	0 0 0	–	0 0 2

BATTING

Cincinnati Reds	AB	R	H	RBI	BB	SO	PO	A
Frey 2b	5	0	1	0	0	1	2	2
Berger lf	5	1	3	1	0	1	1	0
Goodman rf	3	2	1	0	2	1	3	0
McCormick 1b	5	1	1	3	0	1	9	1
Lombardi c	3	1	0	0	2	1	9	0
Craft cf	5	0	3	1	0	0	1	0
Riggs 3b	4	0	1	1	0	0	0	3
Myers ss	4	0	0	0	0	2	0	1
Vander Meer p	4	1	1	0	0	1	2	4
TOTALS	**38**	**6**	**11**	**6**	**4**	**8**	**27**	**11**

BATTING

2B: Berger (3).
3B: Berger (2).
HR: McCormick (2).
Team LOB: 9.

SB: Goodman (1).

Brooklyn Dodgers	AB	R	H	RBI	BB	SO	PO	A
Cuyler rf	2	0	0	0	2	0	1	0
Coscarart 2b	2	0	0	0	0	1	1	2
Brack ph	1	0	0	0	0	1	0	0
Hudson 2b	1	0	0	0	0	1	1	0
Hassett lf	4	0	0	0	0	0	3	0
Phelps c	3	0	0	0	1	1	9	0
Rosen pr	0	0	0	0	0	0	0	0
Lavagetto 3b	2	0	0	0	2	0	0	2
Camilli 1b	1	0	0	0	3	0	7	0
Koy cf	4	0	0	0	0	1	4	0
Durocher ss	4	0	0	0	0	0	1	2
Butcher p	0	0	0	0	0	0	0	1
Pressnell p	2	0	0	0	0	1	0	0
Hamlin p	0	0	0	0	0	0	0	1
English ph	1	0	0	0	0	1	0	0
Tamulis p	0	0	0	0	0	0	0	0
TOTALS	27	0	0	0	8	7	27	8

FIELDING

E: Lavagetto 2 (13).

BATTING

Team LOB: 8.

PITCHING

Cincinnati Reds	IP	H	R	ER	BB	SO	HR	BFP
Vander Meer W(7-2)	9	0	0	0	8	7	0	35

Brooklyn Dodgers	IP	H	R	ER	BB	SO	HR	BFP
Butcher L(4-3)	2.2	5	4	4	3	1	1	16
Pressnell	3.2	4	1	1	0	3	0	14
Hamlin	1.2	2	1	0	1	3	0	9
Tamulis	1	0	0	0	0	1	0	3
TOTALS	9	11	6	5	4	8	1	42

Umpires: HP—Bill Stewart, 1B—Dolly Stark, 3B—George Barr

Time of Game: 2:22   **Attendance:** 38,748

Notes

2 **described Vandy as "mean":** Pesky and Pepe, *Few and Chosen*, 41.

2 **"spine-tingling,":** *Cincinnati Enquirer*, June 16, 1938.

3 **In the fifth inning:** Langford, *Legends of Baseball*, 87.

3 **Picking Cuccinello off:** James, *New Bill James Historical Baseball Abstract*, 383.

3 **Just about the time Cuccinello:** Mathias, *GI Generation*, 224.

4 **As the game moved along:** *Cincinnati Enquirer*, June 16, 1938.

4 **Vander Meer had picked up:** Levine, *Baseball History* 2, 87.

5 **Eighty-three pitchers:** North American Newspaper Alliance, January 6, 1939.

5 **"I was lucky":** *Cincinnati Enquirer*, June 16, 1938.

1. NIGHTTIME PAGEANTRY

7 **Thousands of "haughty gothamites,":** *Cincinnati Enquirer*, June 16, 1938.

7 **"Whether night ball":** *Sporting News*, June 23, 1938.

7 **Teenager Edie McCaslin attended:** McGee, *Greatest Ballpark Ever*, 137.

8 **"I wish Mom":** Graham, *Great No-Hit Games*, 42.

8 **"Watch Johnny Vander Meer":** *Washington Post*, June 16, 1938.

8 **In a brief ceremony:** Pietrusza, *Lights On*, 125.

9 **"Why can't we":** Allen, *100 Years*, 253.

9 **So he did:** Koppett, *Koppett's Concise History*, 190.

10 **The *New York Times*'s Arthur Daley:** *New York Times*, May 31, 1965.

10 **"as something of a charlatan":** Allen, *Cincinnati Reds*, 236.

10 **"That's bush league stuff":** *New York Times*, May 31, 1965.

10 **As he was heading:** Warfield, *Roaring Redhead*, 58.

11 **Stoneham abstained:** Allen, *100 Years*, 252.

11 **"Night baseball":** *New York Times*, May 31, 1965.

11 **Neither were players happy:** Pietrusza, *Lights On*, 108.

11 **Finally, on a cold night:** Pietrusza, *Lights On*, 111.

12 **MacPhail never backed away:** Pietrusza, *Lights On*, 114–15.

12 **Cincinnati played seven:** *Time*, June 27, 1938.

12 **"The directors of":** Warfield, *Roaring Redhead*, 76–77.

13 **"the Dodgers should":** Quoted in Alexander, *Breaking the Slump*, 151.

13 **"Brooklyn will put in":** *Los Angeles Times*, May 26, 1938.

13 **"Brooklyn—the City":** *New York Times*, June 15, 1938.

13 **But Brooklyn officialdom:** Quoted in Rud Rennie, newspaper clipping, undated, Vander Meer file, Baseball Hall of Fame, Cooperstown NY.

13 **"the best lighting":** Pietrusza, *Lights On,* 121.
13 **The *Brooklyn Eagle*:** Quoted in Pietrusza, *Lights On,* 124.
14 **Vandy was used:** *New York World-Telegram and Sun,* January 28, 1939.
14 **"It seems to this":** *New York Times,* June 15, 1938.
15 **The ushers were having trouble:** *Los Angeles Times,* June 15, 1988.
15 **These were the same kind:** *Washington Post,* April 25, 1938.
16 **Owens raced against:** Weinbaum, "Vander Meer's Feat."
16 **"I told them":** http://www.texassports.com/genrel/01107aag.
html, accessed July 1, 2010.
16 **In a broad-jump exhibition:** Baker, *Jesse Owens,* 154–55.
16 **After Vandy and Ruth chatted:** Porter, "1938 Night Baseball."

2. FIRST INNING

18 **"Why, we'll have":** *New York Times,* March 24, 1938.
19 **When the lights became:** Francis, "He Shot the Players."
19 **Frey, whose real first name:** *New York World-Telegram and Sun,* July 22, 1936.
19 **It didn't take "big ears":** Kahn, "In the Catbird Seat."
19 **"When they roast":** *New York World-Telegram and Sun,* July 22, 1936.
20 **When Bill McKechnie took over:** James, *New Bill James Historical Baseball Abstract,* 505.
21 **In his thirteen-year career:** "Frank McCormick."
22 **"and the fellow":** Spector, "Schnozz."
22 **"He was a seven-second man":** Gilbert, *They Also Served,* 62.
23 **"You had been in":** James, *New Bill James Historical Baseball Abstract,* 384.
23 **Lombardi swung the heaviest:** James, *New Bill James Historical Baseball Abstract,* 383.
23 **He would hit vicious:** James, *New Bill James Historical Baseball Abstract,* 388.
23 **"If he were playing today":** "Lombardi, Ernie," accessed July 4, 2010.
23 **When Lombardi came up:** James, *New Bill James Historical Baseball Abstract,* 381
24 **His teammates:** Newspaper clipping, *Oakland Tribune,* undated, Vander Meer file, Baseball Hall of Fame, Cooperstown NY.
24 **The Cyrano name came:** James, *New Bill James Historical Baseball Abstract,* 383.
24 **Sportswriter Roger Kahn:** Kahn, "In the Catbird Seat."

3. BOTTOM OF THE FIRST

26 **But they weren't going to outsmart:** Wilber, *For the Love of the Game*, 141.

27 **"He would stick":** Mulligan, *1940 Cincinnati Reds*, 76.

27 **Lombardi led the National League:** James, *New Bill James Historical Baseball Abstract*, 388–89.

27 **He also could pick off:** Vander Meer, oral history by Austin, December 13, 1990.

27 **As the game began:** *New York Times*, October 22, 1997.

27 **As Vandy went:** *New York Daily News*, June 16, 1938.

27 **The first batter:** "Kiki Cuyler."

28 **The Dodgers' number two hitter:** *New York Times*, March 24, 1938.

29 **Coscarart may be best remembered:** *San Diego Union-Tribune*, July 27, 2002.

29 **"could use a little":** *Washington Post*, June 25, 1938.

30 **His father ran:** *New York Times*, August 26, 1997.

4. A SECOND CHANCE

31 **Johnny received:** Vander Meer, oral history by Austin, December 13, 1990.

31 **The first baseball field:** Wilber, *For the Love of the Game*, 141.

32 **"Back then there weren't":** Honig, *Baseball between the Lines*, 125.

32 **"That's all I did":** Honig, *Baseball between the Lines*, 125.

32 **"If you owned":** New Jersey Media Group, April 29, 1996.

32 **"I suppose it was":** Wilber, *For the Love of the Game*, 141.

32 **Johnny stayed eight weeks:** Vander Meer and Kirksey, "Two Games," 41.

33 **One story has it:** Vander Meer and Kirksey, "Two Games," 42.

33 **In another story:** *Bergen (NJ) Record*, October 7, 1997.

33 **While he was generally:** Campbell, *Ninth Series*, 277.

33 **Johnny wasn't about:** Wilber, *For the Love of the Game*, 141.

33 **During his teens:** Wilber, *For the Love of the Game*, 142.

34 **It wasn't until 1940:** *Paterson (NJ) Evening News*, June 17, 1938.

34 **"I was wild":** *New York Daily News*, June 17, 1938.

34 **The Rangers rarely lost:** Lichtman, *Dutch Master*, 25.

34 **Johnny's parents:** *Grand Rapids (MI) Press*, July 7, 2007.

34 **His father wanted:** Wilber, *For the Love of the Game*, 142.

35 **"I felt . . . if":** New Jersey Media Group, April 29, 1996.

35 **"I guess the good old":** *New York Times*, October 12, 1997.

35 **For three straight years:** New Jersey Media Group, April 29, 1996.

35 **Johnny set his sights:** *Kansas City Star*, May 29, 1983.

36 **"The times were tough":** Alexander, *Breaking the Slump*, 13.

5. SECOND INNING

37 **In the bottom half:** Vitty, "Babe Phelps."

38 **Next up was Harry:** Bingham, "Not Such a Tough Cookie."

39 **Camilli led the league:** "Dolph Camilli."

39 **"a quiet, gentle man":** *New York Times*, October 10, 1997.

6. THIRD INNING

41 **Then Vandy got:** Campbell, *Ninth Series*, 278.

41 **"I've got the very boy":** Newspaper clipping, June 23, 1938, Vander Meer file, Baseball Hall of Fame, Cooperstown NY.

41 **He put forth:** *Paterson (NJ) Sunday News*, June 19, 1939.

42 **Driscoll recommended:** "From 'Wild' Man to Wonder Man," newspaper clipping, undated, Vander Meer file, Baseball Hall of Fame, Cooperstown NY.

42 **Johnny couldn't wait:** Vander Meer, oral history by Austin, December 13, 1990.

42 **"I'll never forget":** Vander Meer and Kirksey, "Two Games," 42.

42 **"Any boy in America":** Ballew, "Johnny Vander Meer Discusses," 244.

42 **"I tried so":** Campbell, *Ninth Series*, 279.

43 **Dodgers manager Max Carey:** Campbell, *Ninth Series*, 280.

43 **Carey relented:** *Paterson (NJ) Evening News*, June 18, 1938.

43 **"I had been":** Wilber, *For the Love of the Game*, 142.

43 **"If someone had":** Vander Meer and Kirksey, "Two Games," 42.

43 **Leo Durocher:** Okrent and Lewine, *Ultimate Baseball Book*, 174.

44 **Reds general manager Warren Giles:** United Press International, June 15, 1968.

7. FOURTH INNING

45 **Catcher Phelps recalled:** Vitty, "Babe Phelps."

45 **"Everybody could follow":** Holmes, "Everybody Follows," 5.

46 **"There were few":** Quoted in Pietrusza, *Lights On*, 112.

46 **The Reds' Sammy Byrd:** Pietrusza, *Lights On*, 112–13.

47 **"I've never yet seen":** *New York Times*, June 9, 1940.

47 **Pitcher Joe Bowman:** *Cincinnati Enquirer*, May 24, 2005.

47 **Even Eastern sportswriters:** Vander Meer, oral history by Austin, December 13, 1990.

49 **Lombardi's groundout:** Graham and Hyman, *Baseball Wit and Wisdom*, 144.

49 **The Brooklyn fans:** Westcott, *Diamond Greats*, 213–14.

49 **"[The fans] knew":** Weintraub, "Legend of Double No-Hit."

50 **"even hard-boiled":** Keller, "Oh, Johnny," 40.

50 **Vandy said he knew:** *Cincinnati Post*, June 16, 1938.

50 **He considered himself:** Honig, *Baseball between the Lines*, 126.

50 **Owner-manager Howard:** Wilber, *For the Love of the Game*, 142.

51 **Vandy worked for as little:** Wilber, *For the Love of the Game*, 145.

51 **Holmes was a former ballplayer:** Becker and Carlson, "Dayton's Wild Duck," 25.

51 **One umpire, Dan Tehan:** Wilber, *For the Love of the Game*, 143.

52 **They received $1.50:** Vander Meer, oral history by Austin, December 13, 1990.

52 **"Don't take that guy":** *New York World-Telegram and Sun*, July 6, 1938.

53 **At Scranton:** Vander Meer and Kirksey, "Two Games," 42.

53 **Vandy was injured:** Campbell, *Ninth Series*, 280–81.

54 **After fifty years:** *New York Times*, June 13, 1998.

54 **His arm still:** Vander Meer and Kirksey, "Two Games," 43.

54 **In his first twenty-two:** *Washington Post*, March 4, 1959.

55 **Nashville offered him:** *New York Times*, June 17, 1938.

55 **In the league playoffs:** *Sporting News*, November 5, 1936.

55 **"We were both":** *Baseball America*, November 10–23, 1997.

55 **At Durham:** *New York Times*, June 15, 1938.

56 **Gooch also helped him:** *Washington Post*, March 4, 1959.

56 **"I can't think":** Associated Press, December 29, 1936.

56 **Newspapers already were touting:** *Atlanta Constitution*, January 24, 1937.

57 **"a great young southpaw":** Vander Meer file, Baseball Hall of Fame, Cooperstown NY.

57 **Vander Meer's showing:** "Debated Final $7,500 Vander Meer Payment," newspaper clipping, undated, Vander Meer file, Baseball Hall of Fame, Cooperstown NY.

57 **During spring training:** *Cincinnati Post*, October 7, 1997.

9. A DREAM COME TRUE

58 **Vandy called:** Wilber, *For the Love of the Game*, 144.

58 **Vandy admired:** Blake, *Baseball Chronicles*, 77.

58 **"I realized a boy's":** Levine, *Baseball History* 2, 91.

58 **"My toughest thing":** Ballew, "Johnny Vander Meer Discusses," 245.

58 **"It didn't take much":** Wilber, *For the Love of the Game*, 145.

58 **Toward the middle:** Lichtman, *Dutch Master*, 38–39.

59 **"Next year, perhaps":** *Sporting News*, July 15, 1937.

59 **Dressen got under:** *Sporting News*, April 6, 1955.

60 **Vandy's record:** *Des Moines Register*, undated clipping, Vander Meer file, Baseball Hall of Fame, Cooperstown NY.

60 **"I walked a lot":** *Des Moines Register*, undated clipping, Vander Meer file, Baseball Hall of Fame, Cooperstown NY.

60 **"I know I'm a":** Vander Meer and Kirksey, "Two Games," 43.

61 **"You can't celebrate":** Graham and Hyman, *Baseball Wit and Wisdom*, 205.

61 **McKechnie appreciated:** United Press International, September 19, 1940.

61 **"You're not a":** Boston, *1939*, 75.

62 **McKechnie also refused:** Boston, *1939*, 76.

62 **"And it was a":** Vander Meer, oral history by Austin, December 13, 1990.

62 **"If you're angry":** Boston, *1939*, 75.

62 **"There's no secret":** Mulligan, *1940 Cincinnati Reds*, 27.

62 **"I'm not going":** January 1939 news release, Vander Meer file, Baseball Hall of Fame, Cooperstown NY.

62 **"Always have an idea":** Vander Meer and Kirksey, "Two Games," 44.

62 **"Look, Hank":** Campbell, *Ninth Series*, 283.

63 **"I didn't even throw":** *Los Angeles Times*, June 15, 1988.

63 **McKechnie changed:** Associated Press, February 28, 1938.

63 **"We don't try":** *Sporting News*, June 23, 1938.

63 **When Vander Meer:** Vander Meer and Kirksey, "Two Games," 41.

63 **McKechnie and Gowdy:** *Sporting News*, June 23, 1938.

64 **But Vandy still:** Reidenbaugh, *Baseball's 50 Greatest Games*, 50–51.

64 **Gowdy then suggested:** Chieger, *Voices of Baseball*, 167.

64 **Who better to teach:** Vander Meer file, Baseball Hall of Fame, Cooperstown NY.

64 **Baseball statistician:** James, *New Bill James Historical Baseball Abstract*, 629.

65 **But Grove saw himself:** *Sporting News*, June 23, 1938.

65 **"I was getting":** Vander Meer and Kirksey, "Two Games," 44.

65 **When it appeared:** *Cincinnati Post*, June 23, 1938.

65 **McKechnie was patient:** Vander Meer and Kirksey, "Two Games," 44.

65 **Vandy always referred:** Honig, *Baseball between the Lines*, 128.

66 **"Nobody thought"**: Carmichael, *My Greatest Day in Baseball,* 145.

66 **"I'll never forget"**: Pepe, *No-Hitter,* 61–62.

66 **As for Grove:** Honig, *Baseball between the Lines,* 144.

66 **"I'll never be able"**: Carmichael, *My Greatest Day in Baseball,* 146.

10. SIXTH INNING

67 **"I've seen guys"**: *New York Times,* October 30, 1965.

67 **"Out of the dugout"**: Durocher and Linn, *Nice Guys Finish Last,* 161.

68 **"There is an air"**: Quoted in Boston, *1939,* 76.

68 **McKechnie established rules:** Boston, *1939,* 85.

68 **"A book manager"**: Williams, "Deacon Bill McKechnie," 89.

69 **But it was that style:** *New York Times,* October 30, 1965.

69 **"He knew how to"**: Bill McKetchnie, quote at National Baseball Hall of Fame and Museum, http://baseballhall.org/quote/mckech nie-bill-0.

69 **McKechnie was a firm:** Vander Meer, interview by Langford, January 10, 1985.

69 **"learned more from McKechnie"**: Koppett, *Man in the Dugout,* 136.

69 **"And that's important"**: Woody, "Johnny Vander Meer's Double No-Hitters," 80.

69 **If McKechnie's career:** James, *New Bill James Historical Baseball Abstract,* 399.

70 **"I don't think I"**: Honig, *Baseball between the Lines,* 129.

11. SEVENTH INNING

71 **In 1938 Vander Meer:** *New York Daily News,* June 19, 1938.

71 **"I make it this time"**: *New York World-Telegram,* January 28, 1939.

71 **"I'd say yes"**: *Paterson (NJ) Evening News,* June 20, 1938.

72 **"You can minimize"**: Honig, *Baseball between the Lines,* 128.

72 **Vander Meer, along with:** *Atlanta Constitution,* April 1, 1938.

73 **"If he wants"**: Newspaper clipping, July 7, 1938, Vander Meer file, Baseball Hall of Fame, Cooperstown NY.

73 **McKechnie also allowed:** Vander Meer and Kirksey, "Two Games," 11.

74 **"Until that game"**: Vander Meer and Kirksey, "Two Games," 11.

74 **General Manager Warren Giles:** Vander Meer and Kirksey, "Two Games," 44.

75 **"I felt I could"**: Campbell, *Ninth Series,* 288.

76 **Vander Meer, losing heat:** Honig, *Baseball between the Lines,* 129.

12. EIGHTH INNING

77 **MacPhail made his first:** Pietrusza, *Lights On*, 103.
78 **The Reds weren't:** Alexander, *Breaking the Slump*, 77.
78 **"Like many other":** *New York Times*, January 7, 2009.
78 **"I was very aware":** Wilber, *For the Love of the Game*, 144.
79 **"I sure did not want":** Rathgeber, *Cincinnati Reds Scrapbook*, 75.
79 **When he took over:** *New York Times*, February 5, 1934.
80 **Ever the supreme showman:** "Crosley Field Historical Analysis."
80 **That was not:** Koppett, *Koppett's Concise History*, 189.
80 **"[The owners] finally":** *New York Times*, January 7, 2009.
81 **"MacPhail believed in":** Smith, *Voices of Summer*, 38.
81 **"And especially on":** Ward and Burns, *Baseball*, 236–37.
82 **"If I stay around":** Graham, *Brooklyn Dodgers*, 155.
82 **Crosley wouldn't stand:** Warfield, *Roaring Redhead*, 64.
82 **MacPhail watched:** Sher, "Larry MacPhail," 61.
83 **"tired of sitting":** *Chicago Daily Tribune*, July 3, 1938.
83 **The Reds picked up:** *Chicago Daily Tribune*, July 17, 1939.
83 **"I'm not going":** Blake, *Baseball Chronicles*, 52.

13. NINTH INNING

84 **"I looked around":** Honig, *Baseball When the Grass Was Real*, 93.
85 **"As the innings":** *Cincinnati Times-Star*, June 19, 1938.
85 **"like a faraway buzzing":** Vander Meer and Kirksey, "Two Games," 41.
85 **"I've got thirty":** Wilber, *For the Love of the Game*, 144.
85 **First up was:** Thorn and Holway, *Pitcher*, 236.
85 **Next up came:** Tepperman, "Goody Rosen."
86 **Next up was Lavagetto:** Bingham, "Not Such a Tough Cookie."
86 **"He fired hard":** Allen, "Bright Night."
87 **"I started hurrying":** Vander Meer and Kirksey, "Two Games," 41.
87 **"What I was doing":** Goldstein, *Superstars*, 195.
87 **"That was scary":** Weinbaum, "Vander Meer's Feat Stands Test of Time."
87 **"I couldn't watch":** *New York Daily News*, June 16, 1938.
87 **"Don't take him out":** Weinbaum, "Vander Meer's Feat Stands Test of Time."
87 **"You're trying to put":** Vander Meer and Kirksey, "Two Games," 41.
88 **"I'll hold up":** Campbell, *Ninth Series*, 292.
88 **"You're either going":** Thorn and Holway, *Pitcher*, 236.
88 **"it was enough":** Vander Meer and Kirksey, "Two Games," 41.
88 **"In life you":** *Sporting News*, May 31, 1961.

88 **Next up was Ernie Koy:** "Ernie Koy Stats."

88 **Lombardi wisely:** Gilbert, *They Also Served*, 63.

89 **All MacPhail could think:** Parrott, *Lords of Baseball*, 121–23.

89 **"Durocher was a loud":** Weinbaum, "Vander Meer's Feat Stands Test of Time."

90 **"From the bench":** Stewart, "They Knew I Had Guts," 45.

90 **"When you cross":** Chieger, *Voices of Baseball*, 109.

90 **"Durocher was the man":** *New York Times*, June 20, 1938.

90 **Vander Meer grabbed:** Cosell, "Vander Meer's Two in a Row," 74.

91 **Lombardi let Stewart:** Pietrusza, *Lights On*, 129.

91 **Years later:** *Cincinnati Enquirer*, June 11, 1988.

91 **"I was pulling":** Newcombe, *The Fireballers*, 130.

91 **Lonny Frey looked:** Newspaper clipping, undated, Vander Meer file, folder titled "The Night that Vander Meer Did It Again, September 30, 1938," Baseball Hall of Fame, Cooperstown NY.

91 **Back in Cincinnati:** *Cincinnati Times-Star*, June 19, 1938.

91 **In Richmond, Indiana:** *Cincinnati Times-Star*, June 19, 1938.

92 **"I wanted a hit":** Frisch, " Fleeting Fame," 28.

92 **"There I was":** Durocher and Linn, *Nice Guys Finish Last*, 103.

92 **"It was what you":** *Los Angeles Times*, June 15, 1988.

92 **"The truth was":** Blake, *Baseball Chronicles*, 76.

92 **"Out and upward":** Pietrusza, *Lights On*, 130.

92 **"John, I blew":** Wilber, *For the Love of the Game*, 145.

92 **"Earlier in the season":** *New York World-Telegram and Sun*, June 16, 1938.

93 **"He caught every pitch":** *Los Angeles Times*, June 15, 1988.

93 **"You never knew":** Zanger, *Great Catchers*, 131–32.

93 **"You know, you're concentrating":** *St. Petersburg Times*, November 2, 1999.

93 **"Vander Meer had more":** Stallard, *Echoes of Cincinnati Reds Baseball*, 16.

93 **"He was fast":** *Los Angeles Times*, June 15, 1988.

94 **"I don't care what":** Ballew, "Johnny Vander Meer Discusses," 244.

94 **"We hit a few":** Associated Press, June 15, 1988.

94 **"Bedlam broke loose":** Quoted in Cosgrove, *Covering the Bases*, 56.

95 **"He couldn't say":** *Paterson (NJ) Evening News*, June 16, 1938.

95 **The fans clustered:** Weintraub, "Legend of Double No-Hit."

95 **Police had to escort:** Honig, *Baseball between the Lines*, 30.

95 **"was never so happy":** *Paterson (NJ) Evening News*, June 16, 1938.

95 **Not only was the game:** *USA Today*, March 6, 2003.

95 **The Red Sox and:** *New York Times*, May 6, 2010.

14. AFTER THE GAME

97 **"They got a":** *New York Daily News*, June 16, 1938.

97 **McKechnie called:** Pietrusza, *Lights On*, 131.

97 **"I cannot tell you":** Newspaper Enterprise Association, June 28, 1938.

97 **"Sure he was great":** *Sporting News*, May 31, 1950.

97 **"It's fortunate that":** Pietrusza, *Lights On*, 131.

97 **"I didn't have":** Weintraub, "Legend of Double No-Hit."

97 **"This screwy schedule":** Newspaper clipping, undated, Vander Meer file, folder titled "The Night that Vander Meer Did It Again, September 30, 1938," Baseball Hall of Fame, Cooperstown NY.

98 **"It was tough":** Allen, "Bright Night."

98 **Not giving the lights:** *New York Times*, September 27, 2000.

98 **In the clubhouse:** *Sporting News*, June 23, 1938.

98 **"Whew!":** Allen, *Cincinnati Reds*, 260.

98 **"I was much faster":** *Cincinnati Enquirer*, June 16, 1938.

98 **"If I'd known":** Buckley and Pepe, *Unhittable*, video included with book.

99 **Harry Hartman:** *Cincinnati Post*, June 16, 1938.

99 **"Fact of the matter":** *Cincinnati Enquirer*, June 16, 1938.

99 **"I was more confused":** Carmichael, *My Greatest Day in Baseball*, 144.

100 **Vander Meer was besieged:** Keller, "Oh, Johnny," 42.

100 **"Baseball is all right":** Pietrusza, *Lights On*, 130.

100 **"and I'm not telling":** "Vandy Shatters Baseball Records," June 15, 1938, newspaper clipping, Vander Meer file, Baseball Hall of Fame, Cooperstown NY.

15. POSTGAME

101 **Vandy arrived:** *Bergen (NJ) Record*, October 7, 1997.

101 **The morning after:** Keller, "Oh, Johnny," 42.

101 **When the crowd arrived:** Newspaper Enterprise Association, June 28, 1938.

102 **"Yes," he answered:** *New York World-Telegram and Sun*, June 16, 1938.

102 **"and maybe the world":** *Cincinnati Post*, June 16, 1938.

102 **Newsmen hung around:** Weinbaum, "Vander Meer's Feat Stands Test of Time."

102 **That afternoon:** *Sporting News*, July 1, 1938.

102 **"Every Saturday morning":** *Los Angeles Times*, June 15, 1988.

102 **That night:** *Sporting News,* January 15, 1939.

103 **Vandy received:** Keller, "Oh, Johnny," 42.

103 **"Nothing like it":** *New York Times,* June 17, 1938.

103 **Lane said he was:** *Cincinnati Star-Tribune,* June 19, 1938.

104 **Vandy was besieged:** Keller, "Oh, Johnny," 42.

104 **"I can't say I'll":** *New York Times,* June 17, 1938.

104 **"I like to pitch":** *New York Daily News,* June 16, 1938.

104 **Reds baseball announcer:** Barber and Creamer, *Rhubarb in the Catbird Seat,* 218.

105 **He hadn't seen:** Barber and Creamer, *Rhubarb in the Catbird Seat,* 219.

105 **Forty-one years later:** *New York Times,* December 23, 2008.

105 **"It's only fair":** *Cincinnati Enquirer,* June 17, 1938.

106 **When the Reds returned:** *New York Times,* July 2, 1938.

106 **FBI director J. Edgar Hoover:** Hoover to Vander Meer, June 18, 1938, Vander Meer file, Baseball Hall of Fame, Cooperstown NY.

106 **"I don't want":** *New York Times,* July 2, 1938.

107 **"Yes, I've learned":** Associated Press, August 3, 1938.

107 **Vander Meer became popular:** Newspaper clipping, June 17, 1938, Vander Meer file, Baseball Hall of Fame, Cooperstown NY.

107 **"What do you want":** Vander Meer and Kirksey, "Two Games," 44.

107 **"If Mr. Giles said":** Vander Meer, oral history by Austin, December 13, 1990.

107 **"that might possibly":** Vander Meer and Kirksey, "Two Games," 44.

108 **"Johnny is taking":** Newspaper Enterprise Association, June 28, 1938.

108 **Giles estimated:** Associated Press, August 3, 1938.

108 **The Reds bought him:** United Press International, June 15, 1968.

108 **"In terms of money":** *Patriot Ledger* (Quincy MA), January 8, 1977.

108 **"Yeah, I've suddenly":** *Des Moines Register,* undated article, Vander Meer file, Baseball Hall of Fame, Cooperstown NY.

108 **Giles went so far:** Newspaper clipping, July 28, 1938, Vander Meer file, Baseball Hall of Fame, Cooperstown NY.

108 **"You bet they do":** *Cincinnati Post,* July 18, 1938.

109 **"deeply hurt":** *New York World-Telegram and Sun,* July 28, 1938.

109 **Giles responded:** *Cincinnati Post,* July 18, 1938.

109 **One of them was:** Gilbert, *They Also Served,* 18.

109 **Pitcher Junior Thompson:** Mulligan, *1940 Cincinnati Reds,* 79.

109 **"a fine kid":** "Debated Final $7,500 Vander Meer Payment," newspaper clipping, undated, Vander Meer file, Baseball Hall of Fame, Cooperstown NY.

110 **"Play-Doh, Formica":** Smith, *Storied Stadiums*, 88.
110 **"I liked Johnny":** Newspaper clipping, July 7, 1938, Vander Meer file, Baseball Hall of Fame, Cooperstown NY.
110 **"Not at all":** Keller, "Oh, Johnny," 38.
110 **"I had seven boils":** Levine, *Baseball History* 2, 86.
110 **In addition to Vandy's:** Crosley, "Conversation with Johnny Vander Meer," 70.
111 **Like many ballplayers:** *Cincinnati Enquirer*, July 10, 1988.
112 **"Remember, all of":** "Debated Final $7,500 Vander Meer Payment," newspaper clipping, undated, Vander Meer file, Baseball Hall of Fame, Cooperstown NY.
112 **Vander Meer received:** Vander Meer and Kirksey, "Two Games," 10.
112 **Over the next few months:** Associated Press, September 21, 1938.

16. THE REST OF THE SEASON

113 **Would Vandy pitch:** Honig, *Baseball between the Lines*, 130.
113 **"Hey, I was hot":** Chadwick and Spindel, *Cincinnati Reds*, 69.
113 **To face Vander Meer:** Associated Press, July 10, 1983.
114 **Sure enough, Stengel:** Associated Press, June 19, 1938.
114 **"I was relieved":** Honig, *Baseball Between the Lines*, 130.
114 **He was so relieved:** Keller, "Oh, Johnny," 42.
114 **William Shambaugh:** *Cincinnati Post*, June 21, 1938.
115 **Giants future Hall of Famer:** Associated Press, July 21, 1938.
116 **"best bet":** *Washington Post*, June 17, 1938.
116 **"It's a wonderful honor":** *New York Times*, July 6, 1938.
116 **"Hey, Johnny":** Crosley, "Conversation with Johnny Vander Meer," 70.
117 **"Just pump it in":** Vander Meer, oral history by Austin, December 13, 1990.
117 **"but those others":** *Washington Post*, July 6, 1938.
117 **After the game:** Vander Meer, oral history by Austin, December 13, 1990.
117 **"He's got it":** Associated Press, July 7, 1938.
117 **"This Vander Meer":** *New York World-Telegram and Sun*, July 7, 1938.
117 **"He's wicked":** *Sporting News*, July 14, 1938.
118 **"It felt good":** Newspaper clipping, July 12, 1982, Vander Meer file, Baseball Hall of Fame, Cooperstown NY.
118 **Paul Derringer:** Wallace, *World Series*, 94.
118 **"You can't tell":** *New York Times*, July 30, 1938.

17. A NEW SEASON

120 **Now listen:** Newcombe, *Fireballers*, 119.

120 **"I am not":** Associated Press, January 24, 1939.

120 **"Well, you never":** *Des Moines Register*, undated article, Vander Meer file, Baseball Hall of Fame, Cooperstown NY.

120 **"Ask me next August":** Associated Press, December 17, 1938.

121 **"has lost his magic":** *Washington Post*, July 19, 1939.

122 **"I still think":** *Sporting News*, July 20, 1939.

122 **"The World Series came":** Campbell, *Ninth Series*, 295.

123 **"I've put my regrets":** *New York Herald Tribune*, November 30, 1939.

123 **"In March, yes":** *New York Times*, March 16, 1940.

123 **"I'm going down there":** Associated Press, February 13, 1940.

124 **"Five in one inning":** *New York Times*, March 16, 1940.

124 **By the end of spring training:** Associated Press, April 9, 1940.

124 **Sportswriters speculated:** Associated Press, April 9, 1940.

124 **"He came back once":** Associated Press, February 12, 1940.

124 **"Johnny has no reason":** *Sporting News*, April 18, 1940.

125 **"There's no such thing":** Mulligan, *1940 Cincinnati Reds*, 79.

125 **"I realize the only way":** Associated Press, June 28, 1940.

125 **Giles agreed:** Werber and Rogers, *Memories*, 184.

126 **Werber also said:** Werber and Rogers, *Memories*, 186.

126 **"Boy, I sure am":** United Press International, August 21, 1940.

126 **"My arm is freer":** *Cincinnati Enquirer*, August 30, 1940.

126 **After winning six:** Carmichael, *My Greatest Day in Baseball*, 147.

126 **"Johnny Vander Meer":** *Sporting News*, September 7, 1939.

127 **In his next start:** United Press International, March 3, 1944.

127 **The decision apparently:** Mulligan, *1940 Cincinnati Reds*, 80.

128 **"I began to wonder":** Carmichael, *My Greatest Day in Baseball*, 147.

128 **"It was true":** Carmichael, *My Greatest Day in Baseball*, 147–48.

128 **"I was still":** Ballew, "Johnny Vander Meer Discusses," 244.

128 **The next batter:** Carmichael, *My Greatest Day in Baseball*, 148.

129 **The team's worries:** Honig, *Baseball When the Grass Was Real*, 132.

129 **"What tickled me":** *Cincinnati Enquirer*, June 22, 1980.

129 **"I'm glad it's all over":** Associated Press, September 18, 1940.

130 **Vander Meer was supposed:** Vander Meer, oral history by Austin, December 13, 1990.

130 **Thompson said years later:** Mulligan, *1940 Cincinnati Reds*, 80.

18. VANDY BOUNCES BACK

131 **"Something went on":** Newspaper clipping, April 29, 1941, Vander Meer file, Baseball Hall of Fame, Cooperstown NY.

131 **But the season wasn't:** International News Service, April 30, 1941.

132 **"I'm just getting":** International News Service, July 30, 1941.

132 **On August 20:** Watkins and Doherty, "Double Whammy."

133 **During the winter:** *Sporting News*, November 20, 1941.

133 **"No club is in":** *Sporting News*, December 4, 1941.

133 **"because he had poise":** News release, January 1942, Vander Meer file, Baseball Hall of Fame, Cooperstown NY.

133 **Vander Meer still had:** *Sporting News*, February 19, 1942.

134 **"so I'd just":** *Sporting News*, August 27, 1942.

135 **In 1943 Vander Meer:** Watkins and Doherty, "Double Whammy."

135 **Vandy had the number:** *Sporting News*, September 2, 1943.

19. THE WAR AND BEYOND

137 **Vander Meer's time:** *Washington Post*, July 6, 1944.

138 **"another year to get":** Gilbert, *They Also Served*, 266.

138 **At spring training:** Lichtman, *Dutch Master*, 103.

138 **Cincinnati was far:** Turner, *When the Boys Came Back*, 94.

138 **"the best pitching":** Newspaper Enterprise Association, February 13, 1947.

139 **"In the years":** Lichtman, *Dutch Master*, 108.

139 **"it's the least":** Quoted in Lichtman, *Dutch Master*, 108.

139 **"The truth of the matter":** Lichtman, *Dutch Master*, 108.

140 **"He had been around":** Peary and Ritter, *We Played the Game*, 35.

140 **Vander Meer wasn't:** Newspaper clipping, December 2, 1947, Vander Meer file, Baseball Hall of Fame, Cooperstown NY.

140 **On June 12, 1948:** Vander Meer, interview by Langford, January 10, 1985.

141 **Vandy's one highlight:** *Sporting News*, June 5, 1949.

142 **The next year:** *New York Times*, February 11, 1950.

142 **Vander Meer reported:** *Sporting News*, March 15, 1950.

142 **"I don't want":** United Press International, March 30, 1951.

142 **Vander Meer apparently:** Associated Press, March 30, 1952.

143 **"I have an old-fashioned":** *New York Times*, March 31, 1951.

143 **"Baseball has been too":** *Sporting News*, April 11, 1951.

143 **"no comment":** Vander Meer, interview by Langford, January 10, 1985.

143 **Vandy wasn't ready:** "Vander Meer Joins Tribe on Trial Basis," April 6, 1951, newspaper clipping, Vander Meer file, Baseball Hall of Fame, Cooperstown NY.

143 **The Indians signed:** United Press International, May 9, 1951.

144   **He signed with:** *Sporting News,* July 18, 1951.

145   **"No job in the world":** Westcott, *Diamond Greats,* 215.

20. A NEW OPPORTUNITY

146   **"A guy has":** *Cedar Rapids Gazette,* June 8, 1953.

147   **From Burlington:** Associated Press, December 9, 1953.

148   **"One thing I'm":** Associated Press, June 15, 1958.

148   **"is far and away":** Werber and Rogers, *Memories,* 187.

148   **"One thing we know":** *Washington Post,* March 4, 1959.

148   **"I remember him coaching":** *Cincinnati Post,* October 7, 1997.

149   **"I don't enjoy traveling":** United Press International, May 20, 1961.

149   **"was probably the most":** Westcott, *Diamond Greats,* 215.

149   **Vandy asked Rose:** Rose and Kahn, *Pete Rose,* 95.

149   **"He was not only":** Lichtman, *Dutch Master,* 120.

150   **"I enjoyed the hell":** Ballew, "Johnny Vander Meer Discusses," 245.

150   **He accepted:** *Sporting News,* July 12, 1982.

150   **On the fiftieth anniversary:** *New York Times,* June 13, 1988.

150   **"He's been run ragged":** United Press International, June 12, 1988.

151   **"I'm a typical":** Reprinted in the *Cincinnati Post,* June 10, 1988.

151   **"I thought Nolan Ryan":** *New York Times,* July 10, 1983.

151   **"The rug has changed":** *Kansas City Star,* May 29, 1983.

151   **"The ball is faster":** United Press International, May 20, 1961.

151   **"We didn't have the":** *New York Post,* May 21, 1996.

152   **"I'll give you a tip":** Associated Press, June 13, 1988.

152   **"I've had the thing":** *Cincinnati Post,* May 20, 1991.

152   **"I am inclined":** United Press International, June 15, 1968.

153   **"No automatic elections":** Newspaper clipping, February 8, 1964, Vander Meer file, Baseball Hall of Fame, Cooperstown NY.

153   **"I don't think he should":** United Press International, March 10, 1964.

153   **"That [a double no-hitter]":** *Sporting News,* February, 26, 1956.

154   **"I had a lot":** *Bergen (NJ) Record,* April 29, 1996.

154   **Eighteen months later:** Coverdale, interview by author, June 30, 2008.

154   **"a loss for the organization":** *Cincinnati Post,* October 7, 1997.

154   **"History?":** Tuttle, *Baseball America.*

154   **"leaves me with":** *Sporting News,* July 12, 1982.

EPILOGUE

155   **Blackwell had an unorthodox:** *New York Times,* October 31, 1996.

155   **"pitches like a man":** Pepe, *No-Hitter,* 66.

155 **"looked like a fly rod"**: Quoted in Neyer, *Rob Neyer's Big Book*, 63.

156 **"the greatest young star"**: Quoted in Robbins, *Ninety Feet from Fame*, 255.

156 **Blackwell was in the middle**: *New York Times*, June 19, 1947.

156 **Blackwell had a superstition**: *Cincinnati Times*, September 7, 1947.

156 **"Sure, that was a"**: Honig, *Baseball between the Lines*, 50–51.

157 **Blackwell retired**: Debs, *Missed It by That Much*, 79.

157 **"can't hit, can't run"**: Honig, *Baseball between the Lines*, 50–51.

157 **Thanks to his**: Associated Press, June 23, 1947.

157 **"I just stood there"**: Honig, *Baseball between the Lines*, 51.

157 **"I'm glad it"**: Peary and Ritter, *We Played the Game*, 35.

157 **"I always thought"**: *Cincinnati Post*, June 10, 1988.

157 **"It's my own fault"**: Reichler and Olan, *Baseball's Unforgettable Games*, 242.

157 **"I was pulling"**: Robbins, *Ninety Feet from Fame*, 255.

158 **Considerable pressure**: Robbins, *Ninety Feet from Fame*, 254.

158 **Houston's Mike Scott**: Scott interview.

159 **Cleveland's Dennis Eckersley**: *New York Times*, June 1, 1977.

160 **"There didn't seem"**: Carmichael, *My Greatest Day in Baseball*, 194.

160 **"I knew I was tired"**: Carmichael, *My Greatest Day in Baseball*, 196.

160 **"You've got to pitch"**: Carmichael, *My Greatest Day in Baseball*, 197.

161 ***Sports Illustrated*'s website**: McEntegart, "10 Spot."

Bibliography

Alexander, Charles C. *Breaking the Slump: Baseball in the Depression Era.* New York: Columbia University Press, 2002.

Allen, Lee. "Baseball's Greatest Achievement." *Sport,* May 1969, 41–42, 89–90.

———. *The Cincinnati Reds.* New York: Putnam, 1948.

———. *100 Years of Baseball.* New York: Bartholomew House, 1950.

Allen, Maury. "Bright Night in Brooklyn." *Sports Illustrated,* June 13, 1960. http://vault.sportsillustrated.cnn.com/vault/article/magazine/MAG 1134505/index.htm.

Alvarez, Mark, ed. *Baseball Research No. 24.* Cleveland OH: Society for American Baseball Research, 1995.

———. *Baseball Research No. 27.* Cleveland OH: Society for American Baseball Research, 1998.

Alvarez, Mark, et al. *The Ol' Ball Game: A Collection of Baseball Characters and Moments Worth Remembering.* New York: Barnes and Noble, 1993.

Anderson, Will. *The Lost New England Nine.* Bath ME: Anderson and Sons', 2003.

Bak, Richard. *Cobb Would Have Caught It: The Golden Age of Baseball in Detroit.* Detroit: Wayne State University Press, 1991.

Baker, William J. *Jesse Owens: An American Life.* Champaign: University of Illinois Press, 2006.

Ballew, Bill. "Johnny Vander Meer Discusses His Baseball Career." *Sports Collectors Digest,* May 25, 1990, 244–45.

———. "These Pitchers Tossed Two No-Hitters in One Season." *Baseball Digest,* July 1990, 60–64.

Barber, Red, and Robert Creamer. *Rhubarb in the Catbird Seat.* Lincoln: University of Nebraska Press, 1997.

Barbour, James. "The Death of Willard Hershberger." *National Pastime,* Winter 1987, 62–65.

Becker, Carl M., and Jack Carlson. "Dayton's Wild Duck." *Timeline,* October/December 2004, 18–25.

Billington, Charles N. *Wrigley Field's Last World Series*. Chicago: Lake Claremont Press, 2005.

Bingham, Walter. "Not Such a Tough Cookie." *Sports Illustrated*, May 15, 1961. http://sportsillustrated.cnn.com/vault/article/magazine/MAG1072554/2/index.htm.

Bisher, Furman. *Strange but True Baseball Stories*. New York: Random House, 1966.

Blake, Mike. *Baseball Chronicles: An Oral History of Baseball through the Decades*. Cincinnati: Betterway Books, 1994.

Bloodgood, Clifford. "The New Red Menace." *Baseball Magazine*, August 1, 1938, 401–2, 424.

———. "Peak Pitching Performances." *Baseball Magazine*, November 1947, 413–14, 426–27.

———. "Rookies Hurl No-hit Games." *Baseball Magazine*, May 1940, 553–55.

Boston, Talmage. *1939: Baseball's Pivotal Year; From the Golden Era to the Modern Era*. Brooklyn NY: Summit Group, 1994.

———. *1939: Baseball's Tipping Point*. Albany TX: Bright Sky Press, 2005.

Buckley, James Jr., and Phil Pepe. *Unhittable: Reliving the Magic and the Drama of Baseball's Best-Pitched Games*. Chicago: Triumph Books, 2004.

Bullock, Steven R. *Playing for Their Nation: Baseball and the American Military during World War II*. Lincoln: University of Nebraska Press, 2004.

Burick, Bi. "Six Pitchers Recall Their No-hitters." *Baseball Digest*, September 1974, 66–71.

Campbell, Gordon. *Ninth Series of American Famous Athletes Today*. N.p.: Grierson Press, 1945.

Cantor, George. "The Rookies Were Kookier Then." *Baseball Digest*, issue 4, 1967, 57–58.

Carmichael, John P. *My Greatest Day in Baseball*. New York: Bantam Books, 1948.

———. "Psychological Boost." *Baseball Magazine*, May 1954, 12.

Chadwick, Bruce, and David M. Spindel. *The Cincinnati Reds: Memories and Memorabilia of the Big Red Machine*. New York: Abbeville, 1994.

Chieger, Bob, ed. *Voices of Baseball*. New York: New American Library, 1983.

Coberly, Rich. *The No-Hit Hall of Fame*. Newport Beach CA: Triple Play Publications, 1985.

Cosell, Howard. "Vander Meer's Two in a Row." *Sport*, May 1959, 74.

Cosgrove, Ben. *Covering the Bases*. San Francisco: Chronicle Books, 1997.

Crepeau, Richard C. *Baseball: America's Diamond Mind*. Lincoln: University of Nebraska Press, 2000.

Crosley, Clayton B. "A Conversation with Johnny Vander Meer." *Baseball Research Journal* 27 (1999): 69–70.

"Crosley Field Historical Analysis." Accessed August 25, 2008. Baseball Almanac.com. www.Baseball-almanac.com/stadium/st_crosl.shtml.

Daley, Arthur. "Baseball's 'Ten Greatest Moments,'" *New York Times Magazine*, April 17, 1949, 14–15, 45–47, 49.

Daniel, Daniel M. "Vander Meer, Rookie of Year." *Baseball Magazine*, August 1938, 389–91, 430.

Debs, Victor, Jr., *Missed It by That Much*. Jefferson NC: McFarland, 1998.

Dewey, Donald. "Major League Maverick: Baseball's Larry MacPhail." *Timeline*, August/September 1992, 30–39.

Dickey, Glenn. *The Great No-Hitters*. Radnor PA: Chilton, 1976.

DiMaggio, Dom, and Bill Gilbert. *Real Grass, Real Heroes, New York*. Zera Books, 1990.

"Dolph Camilli." TheBaseballPage.com. Accessed July 4, 2010. http://www.thebaseballpage.com/players/camildoo1.php.

Drebinger, John. "That Sophomore Jinx." *Baseball Magazine*, January 1939, 339–40, 378–79.

Durocher, Leo, and Ed Linn. *Nice Guys Finish Last*. New York: Simon and Schuster, 1975.

"Ernie Koy Stats." Accessed August 7, 2010. BaseballAlmanac.com. http://www.baseball-almanac.com/players/player.php?p=koyero1.

Feller, Bob, and Bill Gilbert. *Now Pitching, Bob Feller*. New York: Harper Perennial, 1990.

Francis, C. Philip. "He Shot the Players." *Chatter from the Dugout* (blog). http://www.chatterfromthedugout.com/he_shot_the_ballplayers.htm.

"Frank McCormick." BaseballLibrary.com Player Profiles. Accessed July 4, 2010. http://www.baseballlibrary.com/ballplayers/player.php?name=Frank_McCormick_1911.

Frisch, Frank. "The Fleeting Fame of No-Hit Pitchers.," *Saturday Evening Post*, July 8, 1961, 28–29.

Gilbert, Bill. *They Also Served: Baseball and the Home Front, 1941–45*. New York: Crown, 1992.

Goldstein, Joe. "Remembering Vander Meer's Double No-No." ESPN.com. Last updated June 18, 2008. sports.espn.go.com/mlb/news/story?id=3444286.

Goldstein, Richard. *Spartan Seasons: How Baseball Served World War II*. New York: MacMillan, 1980.

———. *Superstars and Screwballs: 100 Years of Brooklyn Baseball*. New York: Dutton, 1991.

Graham, Frank, Jr. *The Brooklyn Dodgers: An Informal History.* New York: Putnam, 1945.

———. *Great No-Hit Games of the Major Leagues.* New York: Random House, 1968.

Graham, Frank, Jr., and Dick Hyman. *Baseball Wit and Wisdom: Folklore of a National Pastime.* New York: McKay, 1962.

Green, Jerry. "Major League Trivia Can Be Habit Forming." *Baseball Digest,* November 1949, 84–87.

Guback, Steve. "Vander Meer Treasures 2 No-Hit Souvenirs." *Baseball Digest,* November 1969, 39–40.

Halberstam, David. *Summer of '49.* New York: Morrow, 1989.

Herman, Mize. "Vander Meer." *Time,* February 19, 1945, 73.

"Heroes of the All-Star Game." *Sport,* August 1954, 22–23.

Holmes, Tommy. "everybody Follows the Ball but dodgers as MacPhail Sells Brooklyn on Night Game." *Sporting News,* June 23, 1938, 5.

Honig, Donald. *Baseball between the Lines.* New York: Coward, 1976.

———. *Baseball When the Grass Was Real.* 1975. Reprint, Lincoln: University of Nebraska Press, 1993.

Isaacs, Stan. "July 25: Double No Hit Vandy Is Seaver's Moon Man." *The 1969 Chronicles: A Sports Writer's Notes.* Accessed May 3, 2008. www.izix .com/stan/index.php?chapter=12&column=3.

Jaffe, Chris. "Ten Most Impressive No-Hitters of All Time." *The Hardball Times* (blog). May 26, 2008. http://www.hardballtimes.com/main/ article/ten-most-impressive-no-hitters-of-all-time.

James, Bill. *The New Bill James Historical Baseball Abstract.* New York: Free Press, 2001.

Jemail, Jimmy. "Was Your No-Hitter the Best Game You've Ever Pitched?" *Sports Illustrated,* May 6, 1957. http://sportsillustrated.cnn.com/vault /article/magazine/MAG1132299/index.htm.

Kahn, Roger. "In the Catbird Seat." *Sports Illustrated,* August 5, 1974. http://sportsillustrated.cnn.com/vault/article/magazine/MAG108 8846/4/index.htm.

Keller, David N. "Oh, Johnny: Forgotten Baseball Legend." *Timeline,* March/April 1999, 34–43.

Kelley, Brent. *The San Francisco Seals, 1946–1957.* Jefferson NC: McFarland, 2002.

Kermisch, Al. "Johnny Vander Meer's Breakthrough in 1938 Not Foretold by Previous Record." *Baseball Research Journal* 30 (2001): 132–33.

Ketchum, Richard M. *The Borrowed Years, 1938–1941: America on the Way to War.* New York: Doubleday, 1989.

"Kiki Cuyler." BaseballLibrary.com Player Profiles. Accessed July 4, 2010.

http://www.baseballlibrary.com/ballplayers/player.php?name=Kiki
_Cuyler_1899.

Koppett, Leonard. *Koppett's Concise History of Major League Baseball*. New York: Carol and Graf, 2004.

———. *The Man in the Dugout*. New York: Crown, 1993.

Kuenster, John. "Baseball's 11 Greatest Individual Streaks in Major League History." *Baseball Digest*, September 2004.

Langford, Walter M. *Legends of Baseball*. South Bend IN: Diamond Communications, 1987.

Lawson, Earl. *Cincinnati Seasons: My 34 Years with the Reds*. South Bend IN: Diamond Communications, 1990.

Levine, Peter, ed. *Baseball History 2*. Westport CT: Meckler Books, 1989.

Levitt, Ed. "Johnny Vander Meer Recalls His Double No-Hitters." *Baseball Digest*, October 1971, 68–70.

Lewis, Allen. "Tainted No-Hitters." *Baseball Digest*, February 2002.

Lichtman, Paul. *The Dutch Master*. New York: Vantage, 2001.

Litwhiler, Danny, and James Sargent. *Danny Litwhiler: Living the American Dream*. Philadelphia: Temple University Press, 2006.

"Lombardi, Ernie." National Baseball Hall of Fame and Museum, Hall of Famers. Accessed July 4, 2010. http://baseballhall.org/hof/lombardi -ernie.

Lowenfish, Lee, and Tony Lupien. *The Imperfect Diamond: The Story of Baseball's Reserve System and the Men Who Fought to Change It*. New York: Stein and Day, 1980.

Marshall, William. *Baseball's Pivotal Era: 1945–51*. Lexington: University Press of Kentucky, 1999.

Marzano, Rudy. *The Brooklyn Dodgers in the 1940s: How Robinson, MacPhail, Reiser and Rickey Changed Baseball*. Jefferson NC: McFarland, 2005.

Mathias, Frank F. *The GI Generation: A Memoir*. Lexington: University Press of Kentucky, 2000.

McEntegart, Pete. "The 10 Spot: July 21, 2006." si.com. http://sports illustrated.cnn.com/2006/writers/pete_mcentegart/07/21/ten .spot/index.html.

McGee, Bob. *The Greatest Ballpark Ever*. New Brunswick NJ: Rutgers University Press, 2005.

Mead, William B. *Baseball Goes to War*. Washington DC: Broadcast Interview Source, 1998.

———. *Even the Browns: The Zany True Story of Baseball in the Early Forties*. Chicago: Contemporary Books, 1978.

Miller, Richard. "Bucky and Duke: Cincinnati's 1939–40 Pitching Duo." *Timeline*, July/September 2008, 18–33.

Mulligan, Brian. *The 1940 Cincinnati Reds: A World Championship and Baseball's Only In-Season Suicide.* Jefferson NC: McFarland, 2005.

Nelson, Don. "Doubling Up." *Baseball Research Journal* 24 (1994): 164.

Newcombe, Jack. *The Fireballers.* New York: Putnam, 1964.

Neyer, Rob. *Rob Neyer's Big Book of Baseball Lineups.* New York: Fireside, 2003.

"Night Turned into Day, Losses Turned into Profits for Ball Clubs." *Time,* June 27, 1938, 28–29.

Okrent, Daniel, and Harris Lewine, eds. *The Ultimate Baseball Book.* Boston, Hilltown Books, 1991.

Parrott, Harold. *The Lords of Baseball.* Atlanta: Longstreet, 2001.

Paul, Gabriel. *My Greatest Day in Baseball.* New York: A. S. Barnes, 1945.

Peary, Danny, and Lawrence S. Ritter. *We Played the Game: 65 Players Remember Baseball's Greatest Era, 1947–1964.* New York: Hyperion, 1994.

Pepe, Phil. *No-Hitter.* New York: Scholastic Book Services, 1972.

Pesky, Johnny, and Phil Pepe. *Few and Chosen: Defining Red Sox Greatness across the Eras.* Chicago: Triumph Books, 2004.

Pietrusza, David. *Lights On: The Wild, Century-Long Saga of Night Baseball.* Lanham MD: Scarecrow Press, 1997.

Poiley, Joel. "Tandem No-Hitters Stand the Test of Time." USA *Today Baseball Weekly,* June 9–15, 1993, 35.

Pope, Edwin. *Baseball's Greatest Managers.* Garden City NY: Doubleday, 1960.

Porter, Ross. "1938 Night Baseball and Babe Ruth Come to Brooklyn." Real Sports Heroes with Ross Porter. Posted May 25, 2009. http://realsportsheroes.com/1938-night-baseball-and-babe-ruth-come-to-brooklyn/.

Prager, Joshua. *The Echoing Green: The Untold Story of Bobby Thomson, Ralph Branca and the Shot Heard Round the World.* New York: Vintage Books, 2008.

"Rarefied Air: What Are the Toughest Things To Do in Sports? Top Athletes Weigh In." SI.com. Updated June 24, 2008. http://sportsillustrated.cnn.com/2008/extramustard/06/12/ten.tough.things/.

Rathgeber, Bob. *Cincinnati Reds Scrapbook.* Virginia Beach VA: JCP Corporation, 1982.

Raune, Tom. "A Retro-Review of the 1930s." Retrosheet. http://www.retrosheet.org/Research/RuaneT/rev1930_art.htm.

"Readers' List: Greatest Streaks by Individuals." ESPN.com, Page 2. Accessed June 10, 2008. http://espn.go.com/page2/s/list/readers/greatest/individualstreaks.html.

"Red Lefthander." *Time,* June 27, 1938.

"Red Stars." *Time,* July 18, 1938.

Reichler, Joseph L., and Ben Olan. *Baseball's Unforgettable Games.* New York: Ronald Press, 1960.

Reidenbaugh, Lowell. *Baseball's 50 Greatest Games.* St. Louis: The Sporting News, 1988.

Rhodes, Greg. *Cincinnati Hall of Fame Highlights.* Cincinnati: Clerisy Press, 2007.

————. *Cincinnati's Crosley Field.* Cincinnati: Road West, 1995.

Robbins, Mike. *Ninety Feet from Fame.* New York: Carroll and Graf, 2004.

Rose, Pete, and Roger Kahn. *Pete Rose: My Story.* New York: Macmillan, 1989.

Rosenthal, Harold. "Vandy Relives Double No-No 40 Years Later." *Sporting News,* July 1, 1978, 32.

Rossi, John P. *A Whole New Game: Off the Field Changes in Baseball, 1946–1960.* Jefferson NC: McFarland, 1999.

Saccucci, Fluffy. "'Dutch Master' Hurled Back-to-Back No-Nos in 1938." *Sports Collections Digest,* November 29, 1996, 140–41.

Seaver, Tom, with Marty Appel. *Great Moments in Baseball.* Secaucus NJ: Carol Publishing, 1992.

Seidman, Eric J. "Catching Up with a 99-Year-Old Veteran." Most Valuable Network. Accessed July 23, 2008. http://mvn.com/mlb -stats/2008/05/03/catching-up-with-a-99-year-old-veteran/.

————. "Here's Johnny: How a Rookie Threw Two Consecutive No-Hitters." *The Hardball Times* (blog). July 9, 2008. http://www.hardball times.com/main/article/heres-johnny-how-a-rookie-threw-two-con secutive-no-hitters/.

Sheinin, Dave. "Ex-Big Leaguer Werber Has Many Stories to Choose From." *Washington Post,* June 17, 2008.

Sher, Jack. "Larry MacPhail: The Man and the Mouth." *Sport,* July 1947, 58–62, 66–67.

Shur, Jon. "Oldest Living Ballplayer Tells All." *Duke Magazine,* September–October, 2008.

Smith, Curt. *Storied Stadiums: Baseball's History through Its Ballparks.* New York: Carroll and Graf, 2001.

————. *Voices of Summer: Ranking Baseball's 101 All-Time Best Announcers.* New York: Carroll and Graf, 2005.

Smith, H. Allen. *Three Men on Third: A Book of Baseball Anecdotes, Oddities, and Curiosities.* Halscottville NY: Breakaway Books, 2000.

Smith, Red. *Red Smith on Baseball.* Chicago: I. R. Dee, 2000.

Spector, Susan. "Schnozz." *Perfect Pitch* (blog). July 2, 2008. http:// perfectpitch.mlblogs.com/2008/07/02/schnozz/.

Stallard, Mark, ed. *Echoes of Cincinnati Reds Baseball.* Chicago: Triumph, 2007.

Stewart, Bill. "They Knew I Had Guts." *Baseball Digest* 14, no. 5 (June 1955): 39–45.

Sugar, Bert Randolph. *Baseball's 50 Greatest Games.* New York: Exeter Books, 1986.

Sullivan, Tim. "Vander Meer's Legacy: A Feat for the Ages." In *1988 All-Star Game Official Program.* New York: Sports Minded, 1988.

Swirsky, Seth. *Every Pitcher Tells a Story.* New York: Times Books, 1999.

Tepperman, Alex. "Goody Rosen." The Baseball Biography Project. Accessed August 7, 2010. http://bioproj.sabr.org/bioproj.cfm?a=v&v =l&bid=2054&pid=12231.

Thorn, John, and John B. Holway. *The Pitcher.* New York: Prentice Hall, 1987.

Trucks, Rob. *The Catcher.* Cincinnati: Emmis Books, 2005.

Turkin, Hy, and S. C. Thompson. *The Official Encyclopedia of Baseball.* New York: A. S. Barnes, 1956.

Turner, Frederick. *When the Boys Came Back.* New York: Holt, 1996.

Tuttle, Dennis. "A Moment's Glory, a Life of Despair." *Baseball America,* November 10–23, 1997.

Vaccaro, Mike. *1941: The Greatest Year in Sports.* New York: Doubleday, 2007.

Vander Meer, Johnny. "How I Throw My Fast Ball." *Look,* August 16, 1938, 8.

Vander Meer, Johnny, and George Kirksey. "Two Games Don't Make a Pitcher." *Saturday Evening Post,* August 27, 1938, 10–11, 41–43.

Vass, George. "Five Unbeatable Records." *Baseball Digest,* May 1970, 18–24.

———. "One Out Away from Fame." *Baseball Digest,* June 1, 2007, 32–43.

———. "Seven Most Improbable No-Hitters." *Baseball Digest,* August 2002, 30–38.

Veeck, Bill. *Veeck—as in Wreck: The Autobiography of Bill Veeck.* Chicago: University of Chicago Press, 2001.

Vincent, Fay. *The Last Commissioner: A Baseball Valentine.* New York: Simon and Schuster, 2002.

———. *The Only Game in Town: Baseball Stars of the 1930s and 1040s Talk About the Game They Loved.* New York: Simon and Schuster, 2006.

Vitty, Cort. "Babe Phelps." The Baseball Biography Project. http://bio proj.sabr.org/bioproj.cfm?a=v&v=l&bid=718&pid=11183.

Wallace, Joseph. *World Series: An Opinionated Chronicle.* New York: Adams, 2003.

Ward, C. Geoffrey, and Ken Burns. *Baseball: An Illustrated History*. New York: Knopf, 1994.

Warfield, Don. *The Roaring Redhead: Larry MacPhail Baseball's Great Innovator*. South Bend IN: Diamond Communications, 1987.

Watkins, James, and Paul Doherty. "The Double Whammy." *Baseball Research Journal* 4 (1975). http://research.sabr.org/journals/online/37 -brj-1975/145-the-double-whammy.

Weinbaum, Willie. "Vander Meer's Feat Stands Test of Time." ESPN.com., Accessed September 30, 2008. http://espn.go.com/mlb/s/2003/06 10/1565923.html.

Weintraub, Robert. "The Legend of Double No-Hit." ESPN.com. Updated April 23, 2007. http://sports.espn.go.com/espn/page2/story?page =weintraub/070423&sportCat=mlb.

Werber, Bill, and C. Paul Rogers III. *Memories of a Ballplayer*. Cleveland: Society for American Baseball Research, 2001.

Werth, Thomas. *Famous Baseball Plays and Players*. New York: Harvey House, 1962.

Westcott, Rich. *Diamond Greats*. Westport CT: Meckler Books, 1988.

Wigley, Brian J., Frank B. Ashley, and Arnold LeUnes. "Willard Hershberger and the Legacy of Suicide." *The National Pastime* 20 (2000): 72–76.

Wilber, Cynthia J. *For the Love of the Game*. New York: Morrow, 1992.

Williams, Joe. "Deacon Bill McKechnie." *Saturday Evening Post*, September 14, 1940, 40–41, 86–87, 89–90.

Woody, Clayton. "Johnny Vander Meer's Double No-Hitters Still Unique." *Baseball Digest*, July 1980, 78–83.

Woolner, Keith. "Aim for the Head: Hidden Perfect Games." *Baseball Prospectus*, April 27, 2004. http://www.baseballprospectus.com/article .php?articleid=2814.

Zanger, Jack. *Great Catchers of the Major Leagues*. New York: Random House, 1970.

Zoss, Joel, and John Bowman. *Diamonds in the Rough: An Untold History of Baseball*. Chicago: Contemporary Books, 1996.

INTERVIEWS AND ORAL HISTORIES

Coverdale, Troy (Vander Meer's grandson). Interview by the author, June 30, 2008.

Frey, Lonny. Oral history by Roger Herz. August 27, 1991. Society for American Baseball Research, Phoenix AZ.

Scott, Mike. "An Interview with Mike Scott." By Ray Kerby. AstrosDaily. com (fansite). Posted February 4, 2002. http://www.astrosdaily.com/ players/interviews/Scott_Mike.html.

Smalley, Roy. Interview by the author, April 20, 2008.

Vander Meer, Johnny. Oral history by Dan Austin. December 13, 1990. Baseball Hall of Fame, Cooperstown NY.

Vander Meer, Johnny. Interview by Walter M. Langford. January 10, 1985. Society for American Baseball Research, Phoenix AZ.

Werber, Bill. Oral history by Walter Langford. October 24, 1958. Society for American Baseball Research, Phoenix AZ.

Werber, Bill. Oral history by Brent Kelly. February 10, 1994. Society for American Baseball Research, Phoenix AZ.